MARKETING

TO

MILLENNIALS

&

GENERATION Z

FUTUREPROOF

The Blueprint for Building a Brand GenZ &

Millennials Love

By

Courtney McKenzie Newell

BOOK DEDICATION

Disclaimer

All the information in this book is to be used for informational and educational purposes only. The author will not account in any way for any results that stem from the use of the contents herein. While conscious and creative attempts have been made to ensure that all information provided is accurate and useful, the author is not legally bound to be responsible for any damage caused by the accuracy and use/misuse of this information.

Table of Contents

INTRODUCTION

Everything to Lose or

Everything to Gain?

There are brands that don't get, brands that try, and then there are the brands that are superstars. The superstars are the brands that consistently increase their market share with next generation of consumers. These brands have cult like followings, always win the popularity contests and are voted most likely to succeed year after year. Their customers are their brand evangelists and help their ideas, products and services spread without having to spend tens of millions of dollars on ad campaigns. Their customers are loyal to a fault and will defend them boldly if anyone speaks ill of them. These brands are what I call FutureProof.

FutureProof brands are the companies that have unlocked the code of understanding how the marketplace has shifted. They have mastered the art of using new school marketing methods. They embrace diversity and inclusion and infuse traditional marketing to create a 360-degree approach to staying top-of-mind. These brands are loved by GenZ and millennials and will not only stand the test of time but will crush it for generations to come.

Today's marketplace is becoming more and more competitive. There are new brands popping up daily and thanks to companies like Amazon and Shopify it is much easier to build your own brand identity and sell online. There's also an influx of social selling via Facebook marketplace and Instagram. There is content overload and increased attention deficit.

To be a brand that is thriving, not just surviving; you must learn how to build a community, not a customer base. You must learn how to tap into the hearts of your customers, not just try to get their dollars, but most importantly you must be human. There is no more B2B (Business to Business) or B2C (Business to Consumer) there is only P2P (Person to Person).

After spending the last decade running a millennial and multicultural marketing & communications agency, I've witnessed countless brands overlook Millennials and Generation Z. I've seen industries hold onto aging marketing methods and refuse to embrace technology, social media or any level of change. I've also seen many brands die because of this thinking. On the flip side I've also seen and helped many brands, including Fortune 100 companies supercharge their brand, and become the go-to favorite in their industry. The reality is the marketing landscape has shifted drastically. Chances are your target demographic not only looks different, but they act and think differently too.

There are books that cover marketing to millennials and a couple that cover marketing to GenZ, but there are none I could find that cover the key differences between these two powerful demographics and how to create a strategy to help you become the MVB (most valuable brand) for both millennials and Generation Z. While there are similarities, these two demographics are unique. Therefore, how you approach them needs to be personalized. Each group consumes information differently, were raised differently and make purchases differently. These groups are also the most diverse groups in history with over 44% of millennials and 47% of GenZ being multicultural. In this book I will share the blueprint for building a brand GenZ and millennials love. I will share my research, survey results, case studies from my proprietary MillennialZ^{TM} Blueprint and best practices from my decade of experience working with brands who want more millennial and GenZ customers. I will share in depth insight into multicultural marketing, how to monitor buying behaviors using psychographics and the step-by-step strategy on how to make your brand FutureProof.

Here's a special note about free marketing resources available with this audiobook.

This is the first time that I'm pulling back the curtains to share strategies that have only been available to my clients; many of whom are multinational, Fortune 100 companies. I filled this book with as much information, strategies, tips and tools as I could. But with the shifting landscape in technology, marketing trends, apps and social media; things are changing so fast I needed a place to keep you updated with tools, trends and techniques. So, I created FutureProofBlueprint.com as a supplement for this book. There you will get access to blogs, videos, podcast episodes and live trainings so you can have the most relevant, up-to-date information as you create and redesign your FutureProof strategy.

Chapter 1:

Your New Customer Base

A consulting client of ours asked me an interesting

question that you might also be wondering. He said,

"What's the difference between Generation Z and

Millennials. Aren't their buying behaviors the same? Don't they want and like the same things? Do we really need a strategy for both demographics?" This question prompted me to write this book. This book will prove to you that Generation Z and Millennials are unique in their behaviors, beliefs and buying habits.

America's minorities are becoming the new majority. Generation Z and Millennials more diverse than any other generations that precede them. They are very connected thanks to social media, and they are more socially conscious. They care about inclusivity and social responsibility, they respect brands that stand for something and they admire transparency. This is why it's so important now more than ever before to have clear messaging on your why. Knowing why you do what you do, who you serve and what impact you plan to make is vital messaging that GenZ and Millennials require. The younger generations are passionate and opinionated and are ready and willing to stand behind brands that are clear on their market position. While there are some similarities, there are also some major differences, we will explore thoroughly throughout this book.

Before we tap into your new customer base, let's look at the four generations so you can understand your target market perfectly.

Four Generations

The battle of the generations is alive and well today. But there are many misconceptions about who belongs in each generation and what makes each generation different from the others. Let's set the record straight. Before we begin, note that each generation does not occur in a vacuum. At the edges of each generation, those members will share characteristics with the bordering generation. When we talk about generations, we are talking about generalities and not absolute facts about each member of that generation. Contrary to popular opinion, not every elderly person is a Baby Boomer. Those born before 1945 are the Silent Generation. The Silent Generation is a small, rapidly aging group, so we will focus on the four main generations of **Baby Boomers, Generation X, Generation Y**

(Millennials), and **Generation Z.**

Baby Boomers

Baby Boomers are the generation born between 1945 and 1964. This puts Boomers in the 55-74 age range. This generation is called Baby Boomers because they were the largest American generation ever born. The birth of the Boomers occurred after World War II. Not every elderly person is a Boomer. Anyone alive today born during or before World War II is not a Baby Boomer.

Baby Boomers make up 76 million of the United States' population. This puts them at 23% of the overall population. Boomers are in retirement or are within a few years of retirement. Due to longer life expectancies, many Boomers are struggling with financing their longer than expected retirement. With Social Security in jeopardy due to this large generation leaving the workforce, many Boomers are losing some of the financial security they had earlier in life.

Boomers have been shaped by the Cold War and the Hippie movement of the 1960s. Boomers are the largest consumers of traditional media such as television. Despite the stereotype that Boomers are not technologically savvy, many Boomers are on Facebook. Boomers tend to have traditional values.

Generation X

Generation X is the generation born between 1965 and 1979. Gen X members are 40-54 years old. While Baby Boomers were named for the baby boom after World War II, Generation X had no such founding event.

They began the trend of being named after a letter, which future generations followed.

Generation X has 82 million members and makes up 25% of the United States population, slightly more than the Baby Boomers right now. Generation X was born during the Cold War and this was a shaping event for them. They are more technologically savvy than Boomers and older generations, as they came of age as the personal computer was becoming popular. Despite the greater digital competence, Generation X still consumes traditional media like Boomers, such as television, newspapers, and radio.

Generation X carries more debt than the other generations, though this is mostly in mortgage debt. Members of Generation X are balancing saving for retirement while taking care of aging Boomer or older parents.

Millennials (Generation Y)

Generation Y, more commonly known as Millennials, are the generation born between 1980-1995. Many older people consider Millennials to be college age and below, but Millennials are actually all of post-college age settling into the workforce and family life. Millennials are 24-39 years old. Some millennials are just now entering the workforce. Others have steady careers, a family, and a mortgage. Because of these differences, it is sometimes helpful to split the generation in half, especially for marketing reasons.

There are 95 million Millennials and they make up 29% of the United States population. Millennials came of age with the internet, so they are much more comfortable in the digital world than their predecessors. The biggest shaping event for Millennials was September 11.

Most Millennials prefer streaming services to traditional cable packages. One reason for this is the rampant financial insecurity of the Millennial generation due to student loan debt. The cost of college has risen over 200% over the last 30 years leaving Millennials as the generation with the most student debt ever. Add in the rising cost of rent and home purchasing and Millennials are far more financially unstable than Boomers or Gen X. Many

Millennials are getting married later in life and buying houses later in life than Boomers or Generation X did due to this instability.

Generation Z

Generation Z is the generation born between 1996 and 2015. Generation Z is 4-23 years old. They range in life stage from small children all the way up to recent college graduates. Perhaps more than other generations, Generation Z is the one most connected with technology. Older members may remember a time before smartphones, but the younger members have always been around smartphones and tablets. Many Generation Z members grew up playing on their parents' mobile devices. They are the most digitally connected generation ever.

There are roughly 72 million members of Generation Z, making up 21% of the population. At the oldest, Generation Z is beginning to enter the workforce. On average, Generation Z members received their first cell phone (usually a smartphone) at 10. They spend several hours a day on those mobile devices.

Despite their young age, many members of Generation Z have seen the struggles of Millennials and Generation X with finances. Generation Z wants to avoid the debt struggles of both groups and be more financially literate at a young age than previous generations. Generation Z opens savings accounts at younger ages on average than other generations.

As each generation grew up, the world was a vastly different place. The post-World War II landscape shifted to the Cold War and personal computer era.

From there, the world shifted to the internet age and the rise of mobile technology. These cultural and technological shifts have had a huge impact on the generations and shape them into distinct cultural blocks. Understanding these generational differences is essential for anyone dealing with other people.

Now that you know more about each generation, we will dig deeper into the two powerful generations: Millennials and Generation Z.

Chapter 2: Millennials:

The Generation That Is

Changing The Business World!

You have certainly heard this word: "Millennials" – a term we use to designate the people born between 1980 and 1995 – who are now between 20 and 40 years old, according to Goldman Sachs Global Investment Research. The precise delineation that determines to which generation you belong can vary depending on your background, so it is not a clear-cut boundary.

What characterizes Millennials?

First, they were born during an age of rapid changes, notably in technology. The name comes from their witnessing the turn of the millennium. Millennials are the first generation to have grown up with the internet and the digital world. According to a Hubspot report over 37% **of Millennials have played a video game streamed over the internet within the past month.** They are also a very informed generation and will analyze and compare their products. This can be explained by their having less money to spend than the generations before, the result of unemployment and smaller incomes. They are also left with heavier

student loans, which also makes them the best-educated generation.

Why are they so important? They represent the biggest generation in US history, even bigger than the "boomers" of the Second World War: we count around 92 million – 25% of the US population, compared to 77 million Baby Boomers. All those people share a common experience of world changes, often revolving around new technologies, which separate them from the previous generations. They are also very diverse and it's difficult to find one common interest, but this is the generation of innovation.

The fact that they tend to stay longer at their parents' (29.9% of 18-34-year-olds in 2010) gives them more

purchasing power for things other than housing as only 23% of young adults were married and lived in their own households in 2012: they can focus on less expensive goods rather than an expensive home. However, the early

millennials are now entering their peak home-buying years (25 to 45 years old), which also leads them to buy the

essentials for their new homes.

But the spending power of the Millennials is growing: if their collective spending power is $600 billion today, it will become more than $1.4 trillion by 2020. It makes them the most significant generation of buyers in history.

What do they do? They have grown with an extensively mediatized pop-culture and have a very wide range of habits and hobbies, reflecting the increasing variety of activities and entertainment of our era. So, they consume more for their own amusement.

As they see the world changing around them, they are willing to shape it their way: 54% of millennials want to start or have started their own business.

Millennials are constantly connected; on average, they spend four hours a day on their mobile phones, mostly on social media, and are more likely to follow tech trends: 2.5 times more likely, to be precise. They also consume online: in the UK, 90% purchased something in the last 12 months. Social media also allows them to follow the accounts that appeal to them, whether they are celebrities, influencers, art or lifestyle. This way, it is easy to target their interests and pinpoint the products they are likely to buy. They like to feel unique and fulfill their personal desires – the Millennials are more than ever a generation that needs personalized experiences.

Lately, being "healthy" has become a magic word, and the recipe for this potion seems to be eating right, exercising, and make sure they feel good in their minds, too. Wellbeing is a rather recent concept: Carol Ryff has theorized the six factors of psychological well-being in 1995 (personal growth, environment mastery, autonomy, purpose in life, positive relations with others, and self-acceptance). In a world where life is more complex and incomes are lower, it is important to focus on your mental health – especially with the images of ideal lifestyles thrown at them on social media. They are in constant pursuit of happiness and are more optimistic than the previous generations. The Millennials sound like a generation that could move mountains – and also shape the whole economy.

What do we learn from this? Millennials have a huge power of influence over economy, overall culture, and changes in general. They are very different from their parents because they master technology and use it as a tool in their every-day life; it is the most influential factor in their purchasing choices and habits. Their focus on wellness opens a new range of trends, and the need for new forms of entertainment. In short: Millennials are the present, and the future of economy.

Chapter 3: Gen Z: The Emerging Wave Of Young Consumers

There is a lot of talk about the Millennials – but what is Generation Z, this growing, young population that will soon overshadow them? There is a blurred line between the end of the "Millennials" generation and Generation Z; the latter starts somewhere between 1995 and 2000, and should end around 2015, though experts do not agree. So, this newest generation's age range is 4 to 24 years old: how can this generation be so significant already when most have not even left school?

What characterizes Gen Z? What is crucial is that Gen Z has bathed in technology and internet from their childhood, whereas Millennials have seen it develop as they grew old. Social media culture is influencing them way more than the Millennials, as they have been in contact with it from their most vulnerable years. They don't know what a world not connected looks like: they have relied on the internet since the beginning of their lives!

94% own laptops, and 3 in 4 say their primary activity for their free time is spending time online. We can say the best way to find them is on the internet. However, don't be

mistaken they are very aware of what's going on online, so they don't share their personal data easily. They are in a quest for uniqueness, so they favor hyper-personalized digital experiences.

Why are they so important? The shift is operating: the population of Gen Z will soon be higher than the Millennials. The oldest of them will have joined the workforce by 2020, so they are getting more spending power; but it is

estimated that they already have a spending power of $44 billion, when most of them still live at their parents'.

Overall, they are loyal to the brands they love, and value rewards programs. They favor quality and don't hesitate to spend more for a better product. And as they spend on average three hours online, they sure know where to look to find what appeals to them.

If Millennials are the most significant part of the population now, it's no good to neglect the youngsters that will soon take their place; but Gen Z don't work the same as our good old Millennials.

What do they do? Gen Z are all about individual expression; they don't want to fit in a category and be like everyone else. They like getting involved in various causes, they believe in talking and not fighting. The fact that they are aware global warming will be affecting them makes them more sensitive to these topics. That's how they differ from the Millennials – they do not focus on themselves but on the whole. Their idealism brings tolerance and opens

society to the future. This affects their consumption: they want to express themselves but also show an ethical

concern. They are in search for truth, authenticity, freedom of expression and tolerance – a very positive way of seeing the world.

Their life is all about right here, right now: their average

attention span is 8 seconds, whereas it is about 12 seconds for Millennials. They jump between activities, multi-task, and are rarely idle as they're always scrolling through their social media feed. Their attention quickly drifts to something else if they are not entertained or interested, so most of the appeal has to happen fast, during the first couple of seconds. Trends are coming and going at the same pace, and they do not linger on something for too long; they need to constantly revisit and discover new things. The logical consequence is that they have no patience. They are used to getting an answer in a fraction of second, getting their new products delivered in less than one day. The fast-paced changes of today create a new world of consumption where everything is at their disposal.

What do we learn from this? Gen Z are the future of

consumption. Even though they are more aware of what they are buying and how this will affect the world around them, they still have lots to spend and are ready to show loyalty to a brand if it does its job right. It is good to bear in mind that social media has a huge influence on them, and even if they have a great critical mind and are kings and

queens of skepticism, it is easy, to create new needs and

appeals in such a diverse world.

Chapter 4: The similarities & differences between Millennials & Generation Z

It seemed like we had only just gotten our heads around the term 'Millennial' when we had a new generation on our hands, in the form of 'Generation Z'.

In an ever-changing business climate where technology dominates and leads the way, identifying and understanding the differences and similarities between these two, tech-savvy generations is crucial. Trends have shown that marketers are now focusing their strategies around these groups of people.

To utilize the opportunities that come with these lucrative, growing markets we need to fully understand who these people are, what are the similarities and differences they have.

Let's start with our Millennial friends, also known as Generation Y (which didn't catch on in quite the same way). They are likely the most studied and talked about generation to date, and yet there's a lot of misconception in the press of what constitutes a Millennial.

[SEP]*"Contrary to popular belief, a Millennial is not someone who was born after the year 2000. In fact, it is widely accepted that this covers those born between 1981 and 1996."*[SEP]

Perhaps unfairly, they are often on the receiving end of backlash denoting them 'entitled', 'lazy' and 'complainers' by the older generations. Don't be fooled, however; they are not to be dismissed as narcissistic selfie-lovers.

Millennials are often cited as being more self-assured than past generations. They also have a strong sense of civic responsibility, a healthy work-life balance and have

socially liberal views.

Why you need to know about Millennials

Let's debunk 'narcissistic, selfie-loving' Millennial myth.
Millennials are the largest generation in Western History
and will make up the majority of this workforce by 2025.

The sheer size of this group means they will dominate the
social, political and economical landscape of our world for
years to come, just as the Baby Boomers have for the last
30 years. This market is a powerful one and is not to be

dismissed.

Who are the Generation Z-ers?

Then we have Generation Z (or Gen Z). This is the
youngest and newest generation to be named. Those who fit
within this segment are cited as being born between 1997
and 2012.

Gen Z is currently characterized by their mass usage of the internet from a young age. They are comfortable with

technology and interact on social media more often that other generations. Growing up through the Great Recession may have given this group a feeling of unsettlement or

insecurity.

Why you need to know about Generation Z

Gen Z are our 'Digital Natives'. They will be the fastest adopters of new technologies, as they were born in the

digital explosion of recent years. As more businesses adapt to the latest global innovations, the more important this

market becomes.

Like their Millennial older siblings, they are also in large numbers, with Gen Z-ers making up an estimated 25% of the population.

Differences between Millennials and Gen Z-ers

Technology

The interesting thing about Millennials is that they are the last generation to experience life before the digital takeover of the 21st Century. They have lived in a world that

pre-dates the internet yet have also led the technological

revolution.

This trait makes Millennials susceptible to the nostalgia of a pre-tech world. You will have seen the returning 80's and 90's trends, including the inspiration for cult tv shows like 'Stranger Things'. These things are targeted at this group more so than any other.

They are tech-savvy and comfortable with mobile devices but have a tendency to still use computers for purchases.

Gen Z-ers, on the other hand, have never known (or cannot remember) a world without digital technology. They have grown up in a hyper-connected world, where a smartphone is never out of reach.

They use the internet to communicate, solve problems, network, learn and make purchases. This is revealing in terms of their buying behaviors and workplace identities. Gen Z-ers are heavy smartphone users, preferring on-demand content, apps and gaming.

Social Media

Both Millennials and Gen Z-ers use social media, but their relationship with it has some distinct differences.

Millennials are the personal content publishers. They are the Facebook status updaters, the Twitter tweeters, and the brand reviewers. They were the generation who first relied on vanity stats for validation, such as likes and comments.

Gen Z-ers prefer a more 'private' social media or

Disappearing Content. Apps like Snapchat are particularly

popular with this generation for that reason. The content

shared on apps like these is not stored embarrassingly, such

an old MySpace profile.

Brand Loyalty

It is notable that Millennials tend to exhibit more brand

loyalty than Gen Z. Millennials will often cite brand reputa-

tion, values and familiarity as a reason for their brand

buying patterns.

Gen Z, growing up with frugal, money-conscious, Gen X

parents, will instead veer towards price comparison and

deal hunting. This can often be a challenge for organiza-

tional leaders in directed marketing strategies. A shift in

focus to UX, loyalty rewards and new technologies is a steer in the right direction to engage this generation more effectively.

Similarities between Millennials and Gen Z-ers

Influence on Spending

As the tech-savvy and digital native generations respectively, Millennials and Gen Z-ers were and are the ones in the household helping older relatives with anything technological, from laptops and mobile devices to social media accounts.

Both generations will conduct research on the internet for things such as holidays and insurance and will use this

expertise to make recommendations to family and friends. They are not only spending for themselves but are also

influencing the spending habits of older generations.

Digital Brands

As both generations have matured in the digital age, they have high expectations for brands to kept up with the latest trends.

Social media communities that encourage engagement from your Millennial and Gen Z followers are a fantastic way to garner the support of these generations. It's also a good idea to make the user experience of your platforms both pleasant and seamless to encourage conversion. There's a reason why digital marketers are so coveted in

organizations today.

Working Preferences

Millennials and Gen Zers have a similar view to their ideal working situation, albeit for different reasons. They both are drawn to the 'customizable career' and are very entrepreneurial.

The motivation for Millennials is more skewed towards finding a good work/ life balance, and to seek opportunities to further learning. Gen Z are more money motivated in their attraction to self-employment.

By understanding what motivates these generations in the workplace, you can gain a better perspective on how to target them through marketing initiatives.

So, there you have it. Two very important generations

already making their mark on the world! The only question remaining is, are you ready to utilize these powerful

markets?

Chapter 5:

New Communication Rules

The rise of internet and social media: new communication rules for marketing your audience

If you want your corporation to be up to date, you have to think like your audience. If you want to reach the broadest audience you could possibly reach, then the best bet would be Millennials and Gen Z, are they are the biggest part of our population. Both of these generations are widely influenced by social media and the internet. To reach them, you must speak their language, and you might find that with internet has emerged new communication rules – which are also used by older generations, despite what we might think.

The main change with the internet and the fact that you can get anything in a flash is that the attention span of people has dramatically decreased. For Gen Z, it is only 8 seconds long. That means you have 8 seconds to deliver your message, or at least to get your audience's interest.

Most customers look for authenticity

Gen Z is the future of our population, and their main quest is for authenticity – they want to find truth and know what is going on around them. That's how "authentic" marketing developed: it's all about not pretending, be transparent, not copying, long-term. It's the opposite of "hype-selling", when a business uses an intensive promotion and it exceeds

the features or benefits the product might convey in reality –
it only leaves customers unhappy and they feel duped.

Check you'll be able to keep your promises and be open to
criticism. Build a friendship with your customers, treat them
like you'd want to be treated. Try to avoid those "persuasion
tactics" and use alignment: offering the right thing to the
right person at the right time for the right price. To do that,
talk to your customers, understand them, suggest new things.
If you approach them in a service-oriented way, your ideal
customers will just come to you.

The quest for privacy

People belonging to the Millennials generation or Gen Z
have grown up with the internet and social media; they are
good at it, and also know about the dangers of such a

platform. So much data is spread on every website they visit,
and they are very careful of what information they share.

93% of Millennials and 95% of Gen Z own smartphones. This tool usually contains their whole lives: bank information, credit cards, personal pictures, all their social media accounts, e-mail accounts, passwords, location data, private messages, home address and professional info... This way, they are very vulnerable: any misplaced tap of their finger and they could be exposed and potentially in danger,

financially or personally.

That is why privacy is primordial to them: they will check if their data is not used against their will, and they are very aware of potential scams, excess fees or data broadcast. You need to create a platform of trust where your customers know their data will be protected. If your system shows breaches, they will likely flee your products and call you out, and you'll lose all your audience as information spreads so quickly.

The era of "social"

This is an era of social media: the ability to be connected with your family or friends, even if you're on the other side of the globe. This has strengthened links between people, but it has also distanced them somewhat. This is an advantage for a business: even if you're based very far away, you're able to reach your audience via those tools.

First: use the social media platforms relevant to your business. It's good to be all over the place, but there are different kinds of audiences on each social media and you don't use them the same way. Facebook is used by the older generations and is more populated by the Millennials backward. Usually, posts with photos or videos have a better impact and are more likely to reach their audience, and giveaways work wonders to earn likes. Instagram is good if you want to boost your products, but you need to give them meaning and set them in an environment that makes sense. Stories are also crucial. Twitter is very convenient to communicate with your customers, you can use humor and it's easy to spread your business if you know what words to use: you might need a community manager.

Second: Continuity and Consistency. If you don't post regularly, you won't get followers – win the loyalty of your audience! Also, repeating your message would help your customers remember it: humans being take on average 27 repetitions to fully integrate a message. It may not work right away but patience is the key.

Third: Stand out. Your post must have a voice, not be generic. Use humor, or a particular design and color scheme, to get people's attention. The attention span of Gen Z is around 8 seconds: your message must be concise and clear, and your first sentence must appeal to them enough they continue reading. Create an identity for your business.

<u>Fourth:</u> Communicate. Interact with your customers.

Organize giveaways so they know they get something in exchange for their follow or like. They might even boast your products for you once they get them. Be reliable, have a customer support or service. Answer their questions, their comments, so they feel valuable and noticed. This is how you create loyalty. It is also useful to take your customers' opinions or criticisms into account. Be ready to change your perception and your plan if customers don't like it.

Social media is necessary for advertisement if you want to get your business out there; nowadays, the youngest and biggest generations don't watch TV anymore, and paper advertisement has proven inefficient for a few years now.

Mobile marketing: follow your customers around

Mobile marketing is a form of online marketing method that aims at a specific target market on their smartphones or any other mobile device through websites, E-mail, texts or apps. With this technique, marketing can be personalized and

directed at a specific time or day or the customers' location. Mobile platforms represent 60% of digital media time for users in the US; using mobile marketing strategically can reach boost your business dramatically. You must first

understand your audience – use surveys or monitor Google Analytics for your site's mobile traffic numbers. Then, set goals – know what success looks like to you. Test your

campaign: is your content mobile-friendly? Does it work on every device? Are the buttons in your emails visible? Can your customers reach you for questions? Provide something personal if you want to reach your customers directly by sending them a notification on their phone. Don't send notifications too often: they might simply unsubscribe.

FOMO: the modern disease

FOMO is the fear of missing out. With social media helping the world to be connected, new trends spread like crazy, and the wish to belong pushes people to imitate each other. More people are getting addicted to their smartphones and social media become a display of their lives. They follow influencers, accounts that inspire them that advertise an ideal life. This creates an obsession for the quest of happiness, or at least to show others that you are having a great life, full of bliss and personal growth.

FOMO usually implies the perception or feeling that other people are enjoying their lives, having more fun and dealing with awesome things – much better than you. By watching those apparently successful people around you, you start to compare them to yourself and think that the grass is always greener somewhere else. It creates a unique sense of envy and has a major effect on your self-esteem. Instagram and Facebook are the nests of this phenomenon, allowing beautiful retouched pictures to be spread across their platforms like an image of paradise. There it is: you feel like you're missing out something fundamentally important. It could be travels, having a luxurious home, living in a cozy wood cabin, sunbathing at the beach, having the perfect body, getting a promotion at work. If you suffer from FOMO, you simply can't stop comparing your life to the others'.

You can easily imagine this envy of other people's lives existing for centuries, as it has been the case. But this is also a very recent and topical problem with the craze for social media and lifestyle. Social media is all about displaying what is pleasant and perfect, because you can crop pictures, show only the bright side of something: basically, it's manipulation because you show only what you want the others to see. It's also easy to hide behind an account, written words,

beautifully staged pictures. Social media are a platform for bragging, faking, lying, and they put everyone in competition for happiness. This makes you question your own life.

This phenomenon is not linked to age or gender, but to lower life satisfaction. If you're highly engaged in social medias, you're more likely to contribute to this negative, self-perpetuating cycle. It can be dangerous and increase depression and unhealthy behaviors.

You can use FOMO positively for marketing with advertisement. If you display a happy and healthy way of life in which your product features, they might just think this is what they're missing in their lives. Sponsoring this kind of lifestyle accounts, or accounts linked to your business can also be profitable, as your audience already envies them, so they would think your product is the key to their happiness.

Emojis: communicating in images

Who doesn't use emojis in a post or messages nowadays? It adds color to your message, but above all, attention. It stands out and brings what you have to say to life. It nuances your statement and allows your audience to understand you better. There is a whole range at your disposal; why not use it? It was a bit cringed at a few years ago when important

companies used them, but today their influence is too big to ignore, and you're missing something if you're not using them.

Even if you want your business to appear mature, emojis can be a great way of getting people's attention. And it appeals to the youngest as well as the oldest: 67% of baby boomers like when businesses use emoji in the right context (it's 76% for Gen Z). Even your grandma uses emoji on Facebook; it's just the new way of communication and 92% of online users use them.

Emojis make your message personalized and stand out, and you're able to better connect with your audience. Your business earns the identity we mentioned earlier. A post without emojis is devoid of emotion. You appear more human if you use them, even if your tweets are programmed. It's a way of entertaining your followers and make your account relatable. But use them carefully: don't overdo it and keep your message clear. Context is key. When you need to be pro, be pro. But keep in mind: Facebook posts having emojis get 33% more comments and shares, and 57% more likes than those that don't – for Twitter, it's a 25% higher engagement rate. Using the right emojis will help you reach a bigger audience.

Goldman Sachs ✔
@GoldmanSachs

How #millennials' life choices will reshape
the #economy: link.gs.com/wu8k 💀 + 📚 =
🎓 ➡ 🚫 👔 🔄 🏠 👨‍👩‍👧 ⬅BACK 🕐 🕑 🕒 🕓 🕕 🕐
💼 🐕 👕 💍 🏡 👶

4:56 PM - 6 Mar 2015

314 Retweets **183** Likes 🟤🔴🟡⚪🟢🔵🟠🔴🟤🟤

💬 84   🔁 314   ♡ 183   ✉

Again: don't overdo it! It might look just like that:

Chapter 6:

Are You FutureProof?

By now, I hope you agree that building a brand GenZ and Millennials love is critical and can be a powerful catapult for business growth. You don't have to search very long before you read about how Millennials and/or Generation Z have ruined yet another industry. A simple Google search will show you numerous lists with vilifying headlines like "We Are All Doomed... Thanks to Millennials." No, seriously, that was really a headline. According to media outlets, Millennials and GenZ are killing real estate, the stock market, retail, banking and yes... even mayo.

These industries aren't dying because of Millennials or Generation Z; the marketplace is simply shifting. These industries waited too long to pivot, which has resulted in their untimely deaths. Social media, influencers, blogs, podcasts, email, text and video marketing have completely changed the game. These "new school methods" have switched it up, for not just you, but for everyone. The brands that are early adopters and get in front of the wave will always be the brands that win. If you were a late adopter, I have good news for you; it's not too late. It will require swift action and an open mind to take action with the things I share with you in this book.

My passion for millennial marketing started in college. I had always planned to go to law school, and I still love law, but somewhere between being the debate team President and being the Marketing & PR Manager for a student organization, I realized that my true passion was in marketing and communications.

During my junior and senior years of college, I held the position of Marketing & PR Manager for the largest student organization on campus. In this role, I was in charge of a 2 million dollar marketing budget and responsible for all marketing of student programming events. My role included everything from designing marketing materials to hiring graphic designers to setting marketing campaign budgets and even booking talent. It was a test run into running my own successful agency.

Two months post-graduation, I opened up my own agency to specialize in millennial and Generation Z marketing & PR.

Over the past decade, I've been a marketing and Public Relations (PR) consultant to U.S Senators, Members of Congress, numerous Fortune 100 companies, hundreds of CEOs, government agencies and startups.

When I started my agency, there were no Facebook business pages and there was no Instagram. I knew Facebook was a game-changer, but Myspace just died a slowed death, which caused many people to believe Facebook would be on the chopping block next.

When I told business owners Facebook was the best way to reach more of their target demographic, many just couldn't see it. They were so accustomed to their way of marketing it never occurred to them there could be a better way.

Adopting new strategies can be challenging, but in business, you either get ahead or get left behind.

Norman Vincent Peale said it best:

"The trouble with most of us is that we would rather be ruined by praise than saved by criticism."

How amazing would it be to have a tribe of customers obsessed with your brand? How phenomenal would it be to have people lined up, excited to buy your product or service? How cool would it be to get inside your buyer's brain and take all the guesswork out of what they want?

You picked up this book because you realize that in order to dominate, you need the mighty millennials and GenZers to not only know about your brand but to love your brand too. No matter how niche your brand is, there is an audience out there who would love your brand as much as you do, if they knew you existed. Even if your primary customer base is not Generation Z or Millennials; as we say in PR, build the relationship before you need it.

Brand affinity is built years, even decades in advance and is often passed from generation to generation. If you think you can wait to market, you are wrong. The key to building brand affinity is to break your marketing down into segments. Each segment will have its own marketing message, possibly even its own landing page, ads and product offerings.

Your marketing segments should have no more than a five-year age gap. This differs from what's being done by most brands. Most brands break down their segments by 9-10 years. For example, segments are typically 18 and under, 25-34, 35-45, 45-55 and 55+. Here's why that strategy is obsolete; think about the top priorities you had as a 25-year old.

Now think about how different your priorities were by the time you were 34. Imagine how much more effective your messaging can be if you spoke specifically to that demographic. In Chapter 11, you'll learn all about psychographics and how to get inside the buyer's brain. Not only should the messaging be different, but often the outlet you use to reach the different segments should be different too.

The messaging should be different because the things that are important to you are different. A 25 year old millennial may not have been thinking about 401K's, life insurance policies and FHA loans, but a 32-year-old

millennial is more likely to be. A 13-year-old GenZer

requires different messaging than an 18-year-old

GenZer. Effective marketing is all about how to tap

into the hearts and minds of your target demographic.

Imagine how much more effective it would be if your

segments were ages 25-30 and ages 31-35 or ages 19-24

and ages 14-18. You can make your messaging so much

more specific and therefore relevant to your target

demographic. You can run multiple ad campaigns

simultaneously to test what messaging is receiving the

most engagement. The key to being futureproof is to

go the extra mile to ensure your customers feel a

deeper connection to your brand. Those deeper

connections are the foundation of a lifelong customer.

Let's do a quick example of segmenting and what that

could look like for your brand. Imagine you've been

selling life insurance for the past decade and you know the breakdown of your customers is 60% male and 40% women ages 50-55. While it's great to make that audience your primary target market. You have to futureproof your efforts. You have to think about where your next wave of customers will come from. You should be looking at how your industry is shifting and how you can best serve your customers for the next 10-20 years. Is there new technology you should be using; are there new platforms you should test?

I'm all about taking the guesswork out of things as much as I can, so one thing we do regularly at my agency for our consulting clients, is conducting research.

It's important to keep a pulse on your existing

customers, I highly recommend conducting internal market research (IMR) at least twice a year. Internal market research is a term I coined years ago. It's broken down into two parts.

Internal Market Research

Getting feedback from your first line of defense. Your employees are the people who see first-hand how people engage with your brand. They see what people like and don't like. They see what and who people talk about and where you're missing the mark. Most companies don't give employees a platform to provide feedback, which causes most employees to keep their mouths shut. The feedback our clients have received from IMR is often mind-boggling to the C-suite because they had no idea how much valuable insight their stakeholders were holding close to the vest.

Some things to consider in your IMR:

- How they feel your company can better serve its customers

- Disruptors (technology, emerging trends, etc.) they see in the marketplace

- Competitors they see as a threat

- What they feel is your key differentiator

- Their favorite brands

- Their favorite platforms and apps

- What they love about the company

Note: Be prepared for negative feedback; you will more than likely get some responses that you're not thrilled about. But remember constructive feedback is how we evolve and will make all the difference in your brand thriving for decades to come.

Some tools you can utilize for your IMR are software SurveyMonkey, JotForm and Interact.

Conducting IMR is vital to succession planning for your business. You must plan for your next wave of customers. This is the essence of being FutureProof. Many businesses think that succession planning is only about planning for the next wave of leadership within the organization. They often have a major blind spot for thinking about their future customers and how they plan to build rapport with the next generation. Many businesses don't have strategists on their team whose main goal is to help them leverage technology, partnerships and systems to help them increase market share and beat out their competitors. This is the lifeline of every business. If you are failing to plan, you are planning to fail.

A core principle of being FutureProof is having the foresight to understand who your future audience is. It's about understanding the next generation. It's about learning how they use technology, how and why they buy and their expectations. Five years ago, if people ordered something online, the expectation was it would take 7-10 days to receive their shipment. Now, thanks to Amazon Prime, anything longer than 2 days is a major turnoff and could potentially cost you customers. Some brands took long to conform to this new standard and therefore lost market share. Imagine how different things would be if Walmart and Target would have offered their 2-day shipping when Amazon Prime was in its infancy. It would've been a game-changer. The larger a company is, the harder it is to implement changes. Smaller companies have more room to agile and disruptive. That is their competitive advantage. I like to think of large corporations as mega cruise ships. If a cruise ship sees a glacier, it's hard for them to pivot quickly. However, if that same glacier was in front of a 10-foot boat, the boat would easily miss the glacier. Some would argue it's because the mega cruise ship wouldn't see the glacier in its path because it's a behemoth. That's exactly my point. No matter how large your company is, you must constantly be on the lookout for what's in your path.

One of our Fortune 100 consulting clients hired my company to conduct our Strategic Market Analysis (SMA) twice a year. We conduct it twice a year, because technology moves at the speed of light, and there are new companies with cool branding and unique product offerings popping up every day. Our client realizes every company, no matter how big or small, has blind spots and areas for improvement. In order to remain on top they need strategists to regularly evaluate their strengths, weaknesses, opportunities and threats.

You've probably seen brands like Nike, Starbucks and Amazon always listed as top brands year after year. You can be one of the companies on the most popular list. You can be a top brand too. It requires change. It requires a new strategy and it requires you to embrace new principles vital to succeeding. There are three principles I'm about to share not only expected by Generation Z and Millennials, but they are also required. Once you understand and embrace the three principles, you too can join the ranks of being an adored brand with more engaged customers who love what you have to offer.

While Millennials and Generation Z have clear differences, three things unite them in what they need to have brand loyalty and become long-time customers. These three things are transparency, authenticity and connectivity.

By the end of this book, you will know step-by-step how to infuse each of the three core values into your company's FutureProof strategy. You will learn all you need to know to become a brand worth obsessing over.

CHAPTER 7:

Rebranding to Reach More GenZ & Millennial Customers

When Does A Company Need a Makeover?

A rebrand may be to have a greater appeal to Generation Z and Millennials. Rebranding can be incredibly powerful for corporate growth, market share, and client acquisition. However, rebranding itself isn't the act that causes growth and diversification. It is the corporate acknowledgment that some aspect of the company is or will be holding back

client acquisition and the bottom line.

Below is a brief discussion on why companies should think about rebranding. Remember that just because a company falls into one of these categories doesn't mean rebranding should be done or is the only answer. It means that rebranding is an option, and a potential opportunity to recharge and reconnect and rebuild your company image. Here are some of the top reasons to consider a rebrand.

Changing Market (Going Global)

Marketing and branding are different if it applied in the United States versus China. This is obvious. So, if a company is going global or at least multinational, is there some aspect of the company that needs to change to be accepted in the new market? A new name or image may be difficult to swallow by current customers but it may make the difference between success in the new market or complete failure. This could even be a reason to rebrand within an existing market. The United States is a big place. The East Coast, West Coast, Midwest and South are all

culturally different places. It may be worth altering your ads and marketing messages to fit in the market better.

Re-Marketing (New Demographics)

Modern markets are truly at the point where established products have been marketing to grandparents, then their kids and even their grandkids. The products have just been around for that long. However, it is painfully obvious there are definite generational differences. For companies to stay relevant from one generation to the next, they tend to change with the times and modernize themselves as needed. Rebranding could be the difference between a new generational market and a slow death into oblivion.

New Management (New Thoughts & Talents)

Often a corporate direction change occurs when new management steps in. This could either be due to a natural retirement progression or due to an issue. Either way, new management brings in new thoughts and new feelings about corporate priorities and ethics. With these changes, the new management tends to want to display those changing to the general public to garner a reinvestment of trust and loyalty. A company's history should not be a reason to hold back management from instilling in the company new thoughts and new ideas. Companies must be able to reinvent themselves freely as corporate management changes.

Update And Outdate Image (Fresh Evolution)

Similar to many items above regarding an aging brand, sometimes a corporate logo needs updating because it is outdated or not with the times. This isn't due necessarily due to the clients changing. It could be due to modernizing technology or an evolving society as a whole. Think of the difference between older and newer cars. A logo showing a Model-T would not be as understood as a logo showing a modern mustang.

Streamlining A Brand (Revitalize A Bad Brand)

Streamlining a brand isn't just about updating an outdated image, it is about correcting a bad image or bad message that is unfortunately or unintentionally being conveyed. Most of the time this is an unintentional occurrence. Maybe the logo means something unfortunate in a different

country, or maybe the name translates very poorly. Further, the logo or brand name could just really be bad, due to a bad hire of a PR company.

Poor Reputation (The New Company)

It seems like every week there is a new accusation of corporate malfeasance. There is constantly something happening that is either shedding a poor light on someone in the management or about the company. This can be devastating for a company's growth and year's end revenue. That stigma can stick around and linger and fester. From boycotts to complete bans, a bad reputation can result in a complete failure of a product line or a company's entry into a market. Rebranding is the attempt to clean the slate and start over. It isn't usually completely successful but is usually better than doing nothing. It signals a corporate's wiliness to move forward and away from the misstep.

Corporate Structure Changes (Mergers)

Rebranding also can be necessary when the corporation itself changes. This can happen when there is a corporate acquisition of another company or product line or a merger when two companies become one. Often the resulting company can send mixed messages about the purpose of the new services or product lines. Rebranding can help reposition the newer company in the market. Further, a company could divide, resulting in at least two smaller entities. In this case rebranding is important to show what the new company does. Shedding dead weight can be good but the current and future clients need to know it happened. Often this means rebranding.

Copycat Conundrum (Identity Crisis)

Another reason, though less common reason, is to rebrand when there are corporate similarities to other companies. So, if two logos or images are incredibly similar, it may be wise to rebrand to show off a corporation's uniqueness, particularly if the two companies are in the same market. This usually occurs when the images used in the logo or certain branding are unintentionally similar.

Rebranding For The Benefit Of The Shareholders

Rebranding is an amazing technique to change the direction of a company's momentum or lack of momentum. It can make or break the client's perspective on the purpose of the change. When done right, a company can reinvent itself, stay relevant and become a new model for the next generation. If done wrong, it can create confusion, distraction, and slight chaos eating away from the bottom line, losing

market share. Rebranding should be done carefully,

purposefully, and with a specific outcome and direction in mind. The more thought and care taken into the action and decision of rebranding the more success the company will see. Be smart, be purposeful, and be bold.

Chapter 8: Reclaiming Your Thrown (Client Case Study)

One of my company's consulting clients is a leading spirits company. We first began working together years ago when they were launching a new flavor to their product line. They wanted to reach multicultural millennials and came to my consulting company to help them create a plan of action. I will break down our process, our strategy and the results that helped our client create their FutureProof strategy.

Step 1: First, we conducted an ACCE Analysis. This is our proprietary assessment and brand audit to evaluate where they currently stood in the marketplace. We assessed all their communications both internally and externally. We also audited all existing marketing, PR and communications, in both print and digital. We analyzed their content design, frequency and channels.

Step 2: We conducted a competitor analysis for their top five competitors. We assessed their likeness and popularity in their primary target demographic and their secondary target demographic. We also conducted an invite-only survey of several hundred multicultural millennial consumers. Our findings were surprising. We found out they came in third place amongst their competitors. We shared with them factors that lead them to rank so poorly. They ranked #6 in a survey of hundreds of multicultural millennials males ages 25-34. Two of the three brands ahead of them in rankings were newer brands that didn't have nearly as much prestige, but still beat them in our findings. All the brands ahead of them in the rankings were utilizing more multi-media marketing methods. They also held regular live activations, partnered with other brands to cross-market and featured diverse models on all their marketing and communications channels.

They were surprised by our findings but later agreed they weren't making as much effort as they used to. They became comfortable and expected the product to sell itself.

Word of advice: nothing sells itself. Everything needs a marketing strategy; otherwise you are gambling and all your employees, clients and partners are on the table.

They were ready to take back their crown and we were determined to help them accomplish their goal.

Step 3: We created our plan of action. Powered by data, we created a strategic communications plan. We leveraged some of what our client was already doing but supercharged their methods by utilizing proven multimedia marketing strategies. We created a digital ad campaign with a custom hashtag and launched our campaign at one of Miami's hottest festivals. We hosted exclusive, invite-only week-long experiences. We upped the ante by creating a mini PR stunt that created a media frenzy. On launch night, we had a line wrapped around the building. We were the #1 trending topic on

Twitter and earned over 20,000,000 earned-media impressions. We did not pay for any press coverage and did not pay any influencers. We had over 4,200 posts about our series of events that week.

To ensure this wasn't just a week of events that only temporarily boosted our client's ranking and sales; we created new brand communications guidelines to ensure going forward their enthusiastic customer base continued to be engaged. We created the strategy for all of their communications to make sure they met my FutureProof M^3 criteria. FutureProof M^3 =Multichannel, Multicultural and Multiplied.

Step 4: We did an exit assessment. We captured the attendee's cell phone numbers and emails. Ninety days later, we surveyed 200 of the event attendees along with the original 500+ people we previously polled. Our results, the brand went from #6 to #2. We re-surveyed another six months later and again another nine months later, right before hosting the next years signature event.

Lessons Learned: In order to FutureProof your brand, you first must gauge where you stand. It's easy to think you know where you stand, but to be accurate you must collect and assess the data. If you have no data to analyze, you can easily start with a survey from your email list, run a contest where entrants must answer questions (remember to keep it short) or you can even host a live event or activation where you can incorporate surveys throughout. There are tons of ways to do this, but these are a few ideas to start.

Chapter 9: The FutureProof Framework

In Chapter 6, I introduced the FutureProof M^3 criteria. I developed this framework after evaluating hundreds of brands consistently listed as a favorite brand by Generation Z and Millennials; while also assessing former leading brands that have either closed or dropped in popularity.

There are three key criteria that brands must incorporate to be FutureProof. Let's explore them each in detail.

1) Multichannel & Multimedia

Having a multichannel marketing strategy is important because you must meet your customers where they are. Multichannel marketing refers to the practice of engaging with customers across multiple channels, providing them with captivating content that inspires them to take action - preferably to buy your product or service on their preferred platform.

Now with so many platforms there are more ways to reach customers, both indirectly and directly. From Instagram to Snapchat, YouTube, Facebook, blogs, and podcasts it's important your brand be where your customers are. Generation Z and Millennial consumers spend three to four times more than single-channel customers. This means you have multiple opportunities to engage with your audience and build familiarity and trust.

Having a multichannel approach helps you remain top-of-mind while also showing your brand's versatility. Your strategy for each platform should be unique and should provide value to users. Deliver your content in multiple formats to resonate with users' preferred content types. Some format types include video, podcasts, white papers, infographics, quizzes, checklists, etc. While it's vital to have a multichannel approach, it's important to know your top 3 preferred marketing channels and content types. Your messaging, tone and frequency should be consistent.

2) Multicultural

Generation Z and Millennials expect inclusivity. It's important to make sure your brand imagery is representative of your customer base. Your content should showcase multiethnic models, groups of friends and couples. The purpose of this is simple. For people to buy your product or service, they must feel connected to your brand. To feel connected to your brand, consumers must see themselves and their friends/family as a part of your brand story.

This first step to doing this is through your content. I can't tell you how many Instagram feeds I audit weekly with only one race represented in their feeds. That is the opposite of being futureproof. It can often isolate those who are not in that group and deter them from patronizing your business. There's a saying, *"You can't be, what you can't see,"* well, I believe, *"You won't buy, if you don't identify."*-Courtney Newell Your brand story should be showcased through the lens of all your customers. A great way to do this is by encouraging your customers to create and share their own content while experiencing your brand, and we call this user-generated content. Repost the best user-generated content and like and comment as many of the other posts as you can. Consumers love when their favorite brands share and like their content.

3) Multiplied

The last criteria in the FutureProof M^3 criteria is to consistently engage. One big mistake many brands make is creating an account on the newest social network only to have it go dormant. No one brand is expected to be on every social marketing platform or to utilize every marketing method. That is virtually impossible. However, consumers should be able to know what to expect from you.

If you know your customers love your Pinterest page and that out of all the social networks you have the highest conversion rate from your pins on Pinterest, Pinterest should be your primary platform. Besides having your primary platform, add two additional platforms and also add an email newsletter to your strategy.

While social networks are great, they present challenges in organically reaching your followers without having to pay for advertising. While paid media is important, it's critical to connect with your customers and prospective customers outside of social media. This is where email marketing comes in.

The goal of all your marketing is to build the relationship with prospective customers, to let them know you exist, about the product/service you provide and to eventually get them to purchase. The best way to build the relationship begins in the inbox. Being able to connect on a personal level with your customers is priceless. You can inform, excite and interact via email. This strategy also requires consistency.

There are brands that are popular within GenZ and Millennial generations who send out email newsletters every morning, while others only send out content weekly. Your frequency depends heavily on your industry and offering. A great way to test what your frequency should be is to allow your customers the option to choose how often they would like to hear from you. Majority wins the vote, but a good rule of thumb is to send out a newsletter at least once a week, and to post on social media platforms at least 3 times per week.

Chapter 10: Multicultural Millennials: Rising Super Consumers

Multicultural Millennials! This isn't just a set of buzzwords, but actually, a powerful and influential market that organizations must know about now.

First, what does this label mean? Who are the Multicultural Millennials?

This rapidly increasing, and often overlooked segment applies to people around the ages of 18-34 who are

African-American, Asian-American, Hispanic and/or Native American. They are estimated to make up a staggering 42% of the 75 million US Millennials overall and that number is growing rapidly. Combined, they are spending over $3.2 Trillion. For context, if that was a GDP, that would be the 5th largest in the world.

This consumer group has carved out their own identity, which is largely influenced by their cultural connections. They are comfortable in different cultural situations and also keep a strong link to their birth culture. They may have relatives living in their home countries, with whom they regularly communicate with, for example. They may

fluently speak other languages and practice cultural

traditions.

With their unique perspectives, there is a bridging effect in the US, bringing different cultures together. With a growing multicultural millennial presence in the major cities, not surprisingly, the above will encourage a cultural shift in consumption for these communities.

The products we buy, the music we listen to, pop culture, trends and much more is being driven by Multicultural Millennials.

According to Neilson's The Multicultural Edge Report[1] *"Multicultural shoppers may be the key to the future, not just because of their numbers, youth and economic clout, but because their unprecedented influence on the attitudes and consumption habits of non-multicultural consumers is upending outdated assumptions and enlarging and expanding the multicultural market opportunity."*

Buying Behaviors

By identifying the buying behaviors of this segment, we can become more efficient and effective marketers. We can take the measures to target these individuals with products and services they care about.

A good example is the food inspired by these diverse

cultures. In this day and age, noodles and burritos would certainly be

considered mainstream; however, there is a demand by this group for more authenticity in these dining experiences to stay connected to their birth cultures. The result is the rise of traditional, independent restaurants and eateries, and

cultural 'fusion' restaurants. Multicultural Millennials are more likely to value cultural experiences that lie outside of their own, which creates a unique opportunity for brands that have a unique offering.

We can even take this one step further in our thinking.

Non-Multicultural Millennials, having grown up

surrounded by these cultural influences, are themselves

"psychographically multicultural."

Psychographics is the study of personality, values, opinions,

attitudes, interests, and lifestyles.

Therefore, their preferences, which are swayed towards

food, products and traditions from other cultures, are also

influential on society. Hip-hop and urban music is an

obvious example of this, as it transcends race and culture.

Relationship with technology

Another interesting way we can, as marketers, study the

potential of Multicultural Millennials is through their

relationship with technology and social media.

It's no secret the Millennials are digitally minded. They are the tech-savvy generation after all, with the majority using smartphones regularly.

The rise of social media has also changed the relationship between brands and consumers, allowing for instant communication and feedback. Millennials are known for brand loyalty, especially if the brand in question engages with them on social media. The way this generation uses social media should also be of interest to brands, as it is a platform to 'showcase their values.'

Multicultural Millennials , in particular, are far more likely to support and prefer brands that support causes they care about. Causes that appeal to this group at a higher rate than their white counterparts include racial discrimination, gender equality, LGBQ issues, environment, and healthcare/mental health. With this in mind, organizations can center entire business, advertising and marketing strategies on these causes to target this segment.

The consumer landscape is changing. Understanding the preferences of this impactful, multicultural generation offers a valuable opportunity to effectively focus your efforts.

Chapter 11: Psychographics –

Inside the Buyer's Brain

Getting Inside the Minds of GenZ and Millennials:

Psychographics 101

Simply put if demographics is the "who," pyschographics is the "why."

It's all about the psychology of what makes a person make a purchase. Let's quickly run through some examples of this.

Let's say your target demographic is millennial parents with some college education and are homeowners with a household income of $75,000 or more. To build brand

affinity you must better understand why they buy, what they buy. This is what psychographics are. It's the buying behaviors of your target demographic. At my consulting agency, we assess and create a Psychographic Persona Profile™. With psychographics, data is key. The more data you have about your customers, means more insight about what series of events typically occur before they buy.

Step 1: Objections

The question you must ask yourself is what are their pain points?

Start by walking through a day-in-the-life in your customer. From the minute they wake up to the time they go to bed. Think through decisions they must make regularly.

Example: take the train or Uber, make coffee at home or stop at Starbucks, cook dinner or order take out, etc. By thinking about your customer this way, you can get to know them on a personal level. Is your customer someone who is willing to spend more for convenience or are they someone who prefers to cut costs wherever they can? Does your customer typically get home before 5pm or do they work longer hours?

A fun way to find out more about your customer is through quizzes. This is a non-invasive and sometimes entertaining way to build your Psychographic Persona Profile. A company that does a great job of this and has become known for its quizzes is BuzzFeed. They have created quizzes like "Which Disney Princess Are You" and "Which State Do You Truly Belong In."

We once created a quiz for one of our healthcare consulting clients titled "What Type of Vitamin Would You Be?," results included a Yummy Gummy Bear, Power Powder Pack, and Invigorating Infusion. It was a very fun way to conduct research on preferred types of vitamins, consumer buying habits and pricing points.

Step 2: Opportunities

The question you must ask yourself is what opportunities exist for me to add value and solve a problem they may or may not know they have?

Based on the objections your customers have on a daily, weekly or monthly basis, examine where there are additional opportunities for your brand to provide a solution. For example: If your ideal customer works long hours and commutes an average of 60 minutes, you may realize that lunch tends to be delayed. They may need one or two snacks between breakfast and lunch. If you sell protein bars or energy drinks, there is an opportunity. Some of the best opportunities come from pain points people didn't even know they had. It takes an integrated marketing strategy to tap into the opportunity. Remember, most purchases are based on emotion, not logic. Consumers make purchases to feel cool, connected, safe, and significant. However, outside of impulse purchases, consumers must be ready to buy. So understanding the objections they deal with and where the opportunity lies, puts you in the best position to capture more of the market.

Step 3: Opinions

The question you must ask yourself is what opinions may be formed about my brand based on our current market positioning?

When consumers think about your brand, what are the first three things that come to mind? Do they think fun, fast, cheap, cutting-edge, high-end, relatable, adventurous? Do they only think of you as a provider of one single solution? Or multiple solutions? Are you an all-in-one solution, a generalist or a specialist? Does what they think of align with how you want your brand to be perceived?

The reality is people buy based on emotion, and use logic to justify purchases. Your goal as a brand is to trigger emotion in consumers. Some people purchase because something reminds them of their childhood or a favorite memory. Others purchase based on status. While others purchase because they can't resist believing they got a bargain.

Companies have been trying to get into the minds of their buyers in increasingly sophisticated fashion for decades. From analyzing statistics of the buying trends of different demographics to envisioning a target buyer for a specific product to using colors in influencing buying behavior, the science of marketing continues to grow in more directions.

All of these things can give companies invaluable insight into where and how to invest their time, energy, and resources. However, incorporating psychographics is perhaps the most controversial, but with the most potent impact on the bottom line.

While concepts such as demographics look at external evidence to predict sales, psychographics gets much more personal, and some would say invasive. A simple explanation of psychographics would be to describe it as personality typing. Whereas other methods would look at race, age, location, and other concrete attributes, psychographics measures cognitive traits such as values, beliefs, lifestyles, hobbies, and emotional triggers. Since there are such vast differences between people within demographic groups, it is reasonable to say that psychographics measures people at a micro-level.

It is easy to see why this arena is so enticing to marketers and with the abundance of social media, it's easy to build an arsenal of data with which to entice the optimal buyers. The various categories that are used to describe people are innumerable.

They can be grouped into areas of interest such as:

Physical appearances: Are your customers into physical fitness, wellness, cosmetics, anti-aging, sports, or weight loss? Do they belong to a gym? Do they go to spas? Do they do yoga? Do they peruse YouTube for make-up tutorials, or, better yet, have such a channel themselves?

Altruism: Do your customers find fulfillment in serving others? Do they volunteer? Do they stand up for social injustices? Do they actively care for the environment? Do they give to charities?

Outlook: Are your customers generally happy and content? Do they often post inspirational quotes? Do they read self-help books or attend motivational seminars?

Relationship-centered: Is connection with family and friends at the core of your customers' lives? Do they frequent cafes and restaurants? Do they often entertain at home? Do they take trips with friends? Are they loners?

Creatives: Do your customers enjoy creating? Do they take cooking classes? Do they do crafts? Do they write songs? Are they itching to publish their first book?

Homebodies: Do your customers do things close to home base? Do they like to eat in? Watch movies at home? Do they like to decorate and/or renovate? Are they HGTV addicts? Do they host dinner parties and do the relatives all come to their home for the holidays?

Since it's so easy to become overwhelmed with the number of possibilities, it might be easier to start more simply. Some basic areas to start are:

- Personality traits

- Activities and Interests

- Principles and beliefs

- Attitudes

- Socio-economic status

- Lifestyle

The political consulting firm Cambridge Analytica created

an infographic that identified the traits of individuals based

on the prevalence of five areas: openness, conscientious-

ness, extroversion, agreeableness, and neuroticism.

		Low Scorers	High Scorers
1	Openness	Down-to-earth Uncreative Conventional Uncurious	Imaginative Creative Original Curious
2	Conscientiousness	Negligent Lazy Disorganized Late	Conscientious Hard-working Well-organized Punctual
3	Extroversion	Loner Quiet Passive Reserved	Joiner Talkative Active Affectionate
4	Agreeableness	Suspicious Critical Ruthless Irritable	Trusting Lenient Soft-hearted Good-natured
5	Neuroticism	Calm Even-tempered Comfortable Unemotional	Worried Temperamental Self-conscious Emotional

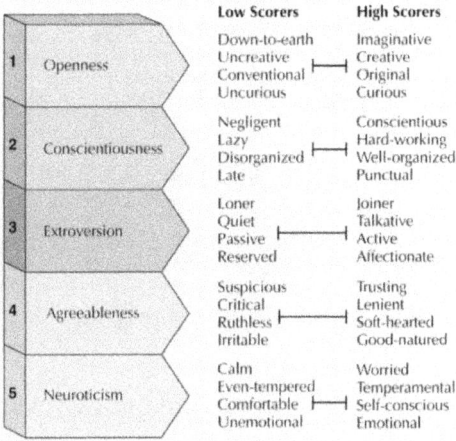

Source: Cambridge Analytica

It is important to note that this is the same enterprise at the

heart of the Facebook-Cambridge Analytica data scandal

for mining data from Facebook without user consent. The

extremely personal nature of psychographics is why it is

also fraught with controversy. How personal information is obtained will speak to the values and integrity of the company.

Some ways that research can be done and data collected include:

1. 1. **Interviewing existing clients.**

   It is probably advisable to choose clients with whom your company has a long and solid relationship. Interviews take time and you are asking for somebody else's.

   Another option is to send out surveys.

   People love to talk about themselves but can be leery of providing personal information for commercial purposes. Be upfront about your intentions of using it to improve your own products. There is the risk that certain personalities may be more willing to provide such information as others, skewing the results, but you'll at least have information about some of your customers.

1. 2. Gather data from website analytics.

The data from behaviors already measured online can help you gather information without setting off alarms in your client base. What has proven the most effective and drawn the most interest on your website? As the saying goes, "Actions speak louder [sic] than words." What has actually motivated people to act in the past might be a better indicator than who they think they are. They may care more about price points than they realized, or they might not readily admit that the color options available for their dream car is more important than they realized.

1.   3.   **Use sites such as Pinterest.**

This can be very time-consuming but could prove well worth the time investment. It simply is not feasible to look at everyone's Pinterest boards, but you could look at those of some of your best or most typical customers.

Though controversies will continue to follow the use of psychographics in marketing, and standards of conduct will always fluctuate to accommodate the new technologies, using such data can empower companies to tailor the methods, channels, messages, and tones they use to connect to each customer. It is in companies' best interests to employ ethical ways of using psychographics to provide the best buying   experience for customers and incite new

innovations.

Chapter 12: What does Gen Z want out of a brand?

Generation Z are not a group of passive consumers. Gen Z wants to feel like they are part of the production process. Gen Z is very willing to give feedback to companies on their products. Gen Z wants their ideas and input to be taken seriously by companies. Often, this feedback will not come through traditional channels like email or a contact form on a company website, but through social media posts.

This means that more than ever, companies must be

mindful of what people are saying about them and their products online. If a member of Gen Z posts about a

product and a potential improvement to that product on Twitter or Instagram, companies had better take notice. If an idea is accepted, companies can create a lot of goodwill by rewarding and recognizing whoever suggested the idea.

This is an example of story marketing, which we will talk about more below. Above all, Gen Z wants to feel they have a voice and that companies listen to them. Companies with a reputation of deafness to Gen Z will fail to sell to this up and coming demographic.

Generation Z also wants to support brands they feel do good in the world. Environmental concerns rate very highly with Generation Z. Companies that pay their workers poorly, have sexual misconduct allegations or discriminate against people due to race or sexual orientation all fare poorly with Gen Z. More than any other generation, Gen Z is aware of the conduct of companies and make their purchasing decisions accordingly.

The Difference Is Real

Brand utility, recognition, and relevancy consistently change with each successive generation. It is like rebelling against the older sibling. It is guaranteed. There will be similarities, but if you don't accept the differences as truly able to affect your bottom line, you're apt to get a straight and loud "you don't know me."

Slight tweaks to your current campaigns can easily be achieved with an understanding of what drives the new Gen Z from their Gen Y older siblings. Gen Z customers and clients are looking authentic interactions with trusted companies that sell products they can show off on their

social media accounts. They need it the products cheaper and easier to so they have plenty of content to display.

Authenticity In Product Use

Transparency has been a hot button issue for multiple

generations of consumers, and Gen Z is no exception. They want to see authentic advertising and authentic branding they can relate to. Products sold for the ultra-rich aren't significant because they aren't authentic to the times and to the people in their communities. A corporate branding campaign should highlight the company's determination and commitment to stay engaged with the real people of the world. Advertisements could include models and actors that reflect more of a rounded vision of the world instead of narrow.

Products could be marketed to a broader audience instead of white and well off. The Gen Z consumer sees the world in all of the colors it holds and isn't contained by the common duality that perpetuates stereotypes and bimodal thinking. The Gen Z consumer identifies more with the fluid nature of being than anything rigid or formulaic.

Authentic and transparent to a Gen Z consumer means that a company not only acknowledges that all people can buy their products but that all people should be allowed to buy their products or services. It isn't necessarily about social equality as it is with millennialism and Gen Y.

It is that Gen Z has already accepted the world as a play on colors and shapes as truth. Any deviation from that thought is only a mark of a past culture.

Trust In The Corporate Identity

Trust in the corporation is the one brand identity that every generation needs and wants. Everyone wants to pick up a can of coke and have it taste the same. Every Lyft or Uber rider wants to ride in peace and not get assaulted. This may seem like a no-brainer, but too often, corporations believe that because their market share is large or the customers are already captured that their brand identity and bottom line can't be affected by an issue that directly influences trust. This is wrong and any corporation that believes it won't be around very long.

A Gen Z consumer needs to trust the company because the Gen Z consumer wants to believe in the company. When they eat or wear or use the product on their social media page, the Gen Z consumer knows that they are doing more than just utilitarian activities. They aren't just covering their bodies with comfortable clothing or providing their bodies with nutrients in the form of food. They are actively advertising the products shown in their Twitter, Facebook, Instagram, YouTube, and Snap posts and videos. If they can't trust the company, they won't be using the product or service. End of story.

When you mold a brand campaign remember that it is not just about the item. It is about what the item means to the company and to the individual. Does the company even like the product or service? It should. If not, then why is it selling it? For money? I hope not. I hope the company is in business because it believes in what it is doing, that it supports building better lives through its products.

Online Exposure

As an extension to the discussion about the Gen Z consumer is online with the company's products. They live online as the first generation that grew up with instant access to smartphones and social media.

These are part of life and an extension of who they are. They gravitate to corporate identities that also live and grow in their space. This means that companies that advertise and exist online and on social media are getting much more exposure than any other marketing techniques.

But it isn't just a form of advertising. It is a state of being.

Remember, the Gen Z consumer views online communities as an extension of their personalities. They can smell an unhip culture from a mile away.

You can't fake a social media profile. You must build a genuine online social media culture. This may be difficult for some industries that don't mix well or with departments that don't have the social media experience. But this is where the Gen Z consumer sees ads, reviews, and recommendations. They follow influencers that are regular people on YouTube and click on ads that target their interests and spark their ideas. Going all in on the digital marketing will grab their attention, and most likely keep it.

It's On Sale

If a Gen Z consumer is going to be posting to social media

multiple times a week, then that consumer is going to need a lot of different products to wear, use, and show off. Though the average Gen Z consumer isn't a cryptocurrency millionaire nor the child of a hedge fund manager. They are average individuals showing off what makes them unique.

Thrift stores are seeing a boom in sales because the Gen Z consumer can shop for less. Not that they are looking for low-quality products that are cheap, but instead, they have no interest in paying full price. If they feel they are getting a deal or a bargain they believe that they can afford more items so they have multiple posts or stories to include in the social media feeds. The online community for the Gen Z consumer is the ultimate show and tell platform.

Offer them the chance to have multiples at a discount or a way to sample different products or services and you will have achieved loyalty. And once you have developed a loyal following, you will have achieved Nirvana.

As we have seen, Generation Z is the future of the marketplace. They are vastly different from the generations that have come before them. Because of these differences, many companies will avoid Gen Z and focus on Baby Boomers or Generation X. This will hurt them in the long run. Companies should have a diversified marketing strategy, reaching Boomers and Gen X with traditional media ads such as television commercials while reaching Millennials and Gen Z on social media. Companies that know who their customers are and what gets them excited will do much better in the long run.

Generation Z is the most connected generation ever and for companies to successfully market to them, they must be more connected than ever. Companies must connect the dots for customers as to why they are in business, why they sell what they sell, and why it matters. Gen Z is much more interested in why questions than what questions. Give Gen Z a brand and a product they can believe in. Charge a fair price. Treat employees and suppliers fairly. Give back to the community. Do these things and Gen Z will come running.

Chapter 13:

5 Ways Brands Can Market to Gen Z?

There are several best practices for marketing to Gen Z. They are authentic storytelling, inclusivity, tech, corporate social responsibility, and social media. We will discuss each.

Authentic Storytelling

The best way to market to Gen Z is through authentic storytelling. Gen Z can see right through traditional advertising, like television commercials and banner ads. They do not fall for cheap marketing tricks. What works for Gen Z is authenticity. Brands that feature real people and real stories do better with Gen Z. This is where storytelling marketing comes into play. Traditional commercials are easily dismissed as fake, but companies that tell the stories of their employees or consumers are seen as authentic and real.

For example, Dove recently moved away from featuring "traditionally" beautiful women (white, skinny, etc.) to featuring what normal people look like. This sort of

authenticity plays well with Gen Z. Ad campaigns that tell the stories of real consumers also work well. Gen Z wants to be part of the product design process. In addition,

involving Gen Z in the messaging for a product catches the attention of Generation Z consumers.

Inclusivity

Gen Z also prefers advertising to be inclusive of all races, body types, and sexual orientations. If an ad does not look like the real world, Gen Z wants no part of that brand or product. Intentional decisions with race and body type of models will make a huge difference with Gen Z.

Generation Z values diversity and wants to use brands that also value diversity. For Gen Z, and millennials before them, a purchase is not just a purchase. A purchase is an opportunity to partner with a brand whose values reflect one's own. To take advantage of this, companies should seek to employ a diverse workforce and have a diverse cast for advertisements. Again, this must reflect the value of authenticity. A token minority person will not be authentic. Companies must actually and actively want diversity.

Tech

As Generation Z is the most connected generation ever, it is essential that companies master the technological piece of business. First, if a company has brick-and-mortar stores, a strong WIFI connection is a must. It may seem counterintuitive to have brick-and-mortar locations for the most connected generation ever, but many members of Gen

Z appreciate the physical shopping experience. Gen Z wants to be connected at all times, and a lack of WIFI is a big hindrance to that connection. If there is no WIFI or if the WIFI has a poor connection or is hard to connect to, Gen Z will find other places to shop.

Some managers may scoff at the added expense of WIFI in a store, but it is an expense that is essential to pay.

Customers who can connect with the outside world from within a store act as unofficial brand ambassadors. Store managers should make sure that their stores are social

media-ready. Keep the inventory organized and

uncluttered. Create spaces in the store that beg for social media sharing, whether that be funny, empowering, or

exciting signage, promotions for social media sharing, Snapchat codes for scanning, or any number of ways to connect with Generation Z customers on their smartphones in the store. If you get them sharing, you will create a reputation as a Gen Z friendly company and that will pay off in a big way.

In addition to cash and credit card transactions, make sure your stores are equipped to handle a variety of mobile payments. Again, Gen Z is the most connected generation ever and are far more likely to have their payment information saved on their phone than they are to carry cash or a credit card.

Allowing for more ways to pay will lead to more sales than simple cash or card transactions.

It is also essential for companies to have a strong inventory management system with information available to consumers through a website or an app. There is nothing Gen Z likes less than thinking a product is in stock but it is sold out. Perfect the inventory management system and let

Gen Z browse your collection online. This will drive traffic to stores and increase sales.

Corporate Social Responsibility

Generation Z is watching. Like we said earlier, a purchase is not just a purchase anymore. A purchase is a statement that the purchaser supports what a company or brand is

doing. This starts in house. Companies and brands that treat their employees well will have high employee loyalty, but it can have an impact with consumers as well. Changes are you probably employ friends or family members of your

consumers. If they know that their friends and family are being ill-treated at work, this will affect their purchasing decisions. Corporate Social Responsibility begins with one's own employees.

This extends to the sourcing and manufacturing of products. Gen Z cares about ethical and sustainable practices up and down the supply chain. If you utilize underpaid or child labor, Gen Z will avoid your brand like the plague. Work with your suppliers and distributors to make sure everyone in the supply chain is being treated fairly and equitably. Gen Z will pay a small premium for this sort of ethical behavior. This is also a tremendous opportunity to share the stories of employees, whether a farmer in Central America or a factory working in China. Treat these people well and tell their stories. Be a brand that cares about people and share these people's stories. This is a slam dunk marketing campaign that will work well with Gen Z. Make sure that everything is done authentically, however. If Gen Z catches a whiff of inauthenticity, then the campaign is a waste.

Being a company that gives back is also a value Gen Z seeks after in the brands it shops. Donations to charity, specifically ones with concerns closely aligned with Gen Z, will create goodwill toward your brand. Environmental concerns, income inequality, and diversity and inclusion are all issues Gen Z cares about.

Maximize Social Media

Social media is where Gen Z is so that is where companies need to go to reach them. Facebook is not popular with Gen Z, especially because Baby Boomers and Generation X are use the platform in vast numbers. The three most popular social media platforms for Gen Z are Instagram, Snapchat, and YouTube and a quick coming 4th favorite is TikTok. These platforms give businesses plenty of opportunities to engage with Generation Z.

On Instagram and Snapchat, brands can feature pictures and videos which promote their brand. These posts should be storytelling marketing. Posts that feature members of Generation Z talking about your products will perform the best. On Youtube, brands can post longer-form content to connect with customers. By longer form, we mean under five minutes. Most members of Gen Z have shorter attention spans and will not watch an hour-long ad about laundry detergent, no matter how good the storytelling. YouTube content should focus on sustainability and corporate social responsibility. Create two-minute videos of how your brand gives back. Play these videos as ads before videos popular with Gen Z.

Another tip is to utilize social media influencers. Gen Z has a higher view of social media influencers than they do traditional television commercials. A look at the main hashtags (#) in your industry on a given social media

platform will bring up people who are influencers who may be good brand ambassadors for your company. Getting these people to endorse your products is a great way to reach Gen Z.

Ch 14: What Millennials Want from Brands

Millennials are a demographic that is hard to influence with traditional brand communication and who are very specific about what they want. If you are targeting this generation, traditional marketing methods and having the lowest prices will not be enough to win them over. However, this is a group you will want to connect with.

Business Insider states that in 2019 millennials had the most buying power. This trend is set to continue until they are overtaken by Gen Z in approximately 5 years.

Why They Are Important to Your Brand In 2020

The majority of millennials are entering their prime spending years and are becoming more and more financially stable. The average age of millennials is going to be 30 in 2020, and this means they are more likely to buy into your products and brands. This makes them your most important consumer market for the coming year.

A lot of research has gone into the retail habits of this generation and it has found they are less trusting of the experts on brand websites. They are more likely to turn to social media and influencers to get an idea of what they are buying. This change in focus has led to a need to change marketing strategies.

If you can truly understand this generation, you will see serious benefits for your business. If you are finding this hard, you must break down the mystery surrounding their habits. There are 5 action points you can use to help you target the millennial market and maximize your marketing to this group.

Brand Loyalty

Like other generations, millennials want products that are well-priced and reliable, but this may not be enough. If you want to generate loyalty from this generation, you must engage with them on an individual level and in small groups through 2-way communications. Doing this will help you build a strong relationship with them and a community that puts the consumer a position to shape the future of your brand.

According to surveys, 68% of millennials will have a few brands they will turn to first to buy which highlights the importance of brand loyalty. They also want the opportunity to interact with brands through brand collaboration on social media or through a simple acknowledgment their feedback has been heard. It is vital that you take on what they have said about their experience with your business because it can benefit your brand greatly.

Encourage Reviews

When making purchases, millennials are influenced by their peers and social media. This is why you must encourage reviews of your brand. This not only helps build your relationship, but you will also create influence in their network.

Fortunately, millennials are more willing to share their opinion online than other generations and will talk about the merits of products. Before buying any products, 50% of millennials will look for opinions of the brand on social media compared to only 35% of boomers. Millennials also feel they influence the purchasing decisions of approximately 4 friends and family members which highlights how they can work as a cross-generational influencer for your business. To benefit from all this, you must actively encourage reviews from every customer regardless of the size of the purchase. The review can be left on your website or any of your social media accounts.

Social Media

When it comes to the marketing messages and brand communications you create, you have to resonate with the customer and stay true to your overall brand identity. The same visual stimulus can be used for millennials as older generations, but the reactions you get will differ. When targeting the millennial market, you need to convey your messages authentically as this reflects the beliefs, attitudes and preferences of this generation. To do this, you need to leverage the known millennial traits to create purchasing intent.

Millennials will look for information about brand identity through social media posts. They will consider if the brand is selling its aesthetic or is there more about written content that describes the brand. If you alter your brand messaging on social media, you will increase interest from millennials.

It is vital that you take the time to engage with potential consumers as well. Millennials will be more likely to like or follow your account if they have intent to purchase from you in the near future. You can guarantee this by regularly posting and interacting with them.

Business Ethics

This is a controversial point, even among millennials, but you should still know about it. It does not matter what

social, ethical or political views you have, you need to think about whether they will help or hinder your business. You have to consider if the wrong public political position will hurt your brand with this demographic.

Around 38% of millennials state they pay a lot of attention to the political and ethical matters related to companies they buy from. If you are selling high-quality and luxurious fur coats, but a lot of issues around animal welfare are

circulating, are you going to sell to millennials? The answer is probably not. Consider the ethical problems you could run into, and promote your brand in a way that lines up with the values of this generation.

Being Authentic

Millennials want brands to be real instead of perfect. The past ideology of industry perfection has dissipated over the years and is replaced with the need for something unique that people can relate to. You should never try to be

something that you are not because consumers will see through this and think your brand is untrustworthy.

With the market as crowded as it is, being authentic can make you stand out and will give your brand the substance it needs to sell. If you have problems conveying your authenticity to the public, try sharing business goals or your mission statement online. You also need to get to know your market and their desires through social media, YouTube and blogs.

Be real. Be charitable. Be consistent.

Chapter 15: The 3 Rules For Success for Marketing to Gen Z and Millennials

Why Are There Only 3 Rules?

Because there aren't really any rules, yet at the same time there are infinite rules.

Overstatement to say the least. Transparency, authenticity, and connectivity are a play on the most fundamental rules that govern all of society. However, rules must be

reimagined for each successive generation as each

generation discusses life, love, and art differently.

Hence, each generation will have its own set of rules

creating an infinite list.

Yet, if they all come back to the basic uncontrollable

human condition can you really say there are any at all?

Yes, because it is a preposterous notion that the continued

success and reliable growth is based on mere chance.

Employers and leaders need some base understanding of

what drives people to follow, to commit, and to stay

brand/corporate loyal. Continued corporate relevance to the

employed workforce is built on the back of a focused

corporate book of ethics.

Those ethics may not relate to morals or even support

fairness or equality. Instead, the basics of corporate ethics

are rooted in decisions on how the firm grows under the

current politics of culture.

Culture is divided into three broad thoughts: 1) how you

view the world around you; 2) how you view yourself; and

3) how the world talks to you.

In today's culture, these three broad thoughts are called transparency, authenticity, and connectivity. In prior generations, transparency was more akin to corporate trust; authenticity was more akin to commitment to hard work, and connectivity was more akin to clocking in forty hours. The word may change with time but the base thought stays.

Each generation will place a significance on a different aspect of life that skews the filter a bit, changing the tone of the broad thought. Take these rules and heed a warning: you are either fully engaged with your rules for success or not at all.

Rule 1: Don't Hide The Truth And Be Proactive On Being Fully Open.

Older generations viewed the first broad thought (how you view the world around you) as a singular trust in the system. There was no need to see behind the curtain. However, younger generations don't trust the "system." They see corporate greed and inequality as driving corporate decisions and choices rather than running a firm to benefit the

customers and clients. The younger generation wants

transparency because an open book shows the true intent. If you truly expect to succeed, then transparency on purpose and actions is critical to trust, engagement, and motivation.

Transparency Improves Corporate Engagement

Once employees and colleagues understand the bigger

picture and their place in the corporate structure, they are more engaged. They can see how the company should change for the better. They will begin to not only

understand their place but believe in the work they have.

Transparency Improves Corporate Trust

In order to avoid the pitfalls of becoming a firm that looks like a shareholder first company, firms must develop improved transparency guidelines. Improved transparency in the corporate decision-making process allows the employee to understand the motivations behind the decision. The

employee will be able to connect the decision and the

decision-making process to the ethics of the firm. The

employee will grow to trust the firm and trust they are not only doing what is right for the shareholders but also the employees and the clients.

Transparency Improves Corporate Motivation

Once employees are more trusting and engaging with the firm, the employees will be more motivated to be a proactive and productive member of the team. They will see the benefits of staying positive about the growth of the firm and will want to participate in its success. An employee that wants to see the firm succeed is an employee that will stay and be motivated to help grow the firm.

Authenticity And The Search For The Self

Rule 2: The Authentic Self Is Based In Honesty And Integrity

You can't force a deal. No matter how great a deal seems if it isn't working out you can't force it. However, many

people love forcing the deal and suffer because of it. Decisions must be made with an acknowledgement of honesty and integrity.

Corporate ethics must focus on staying true to the purpose of the company and the commitment to client and customer satisfaction. Is this action a correct one? Is this decision

being made at the right time? Allow yourself, your colleagues, and your employees to be honest about current actions and future possibilities. Allow the decision making process to be primarily driven by integrity and honor. If you are true to yourself and your corporate vision of ethics, your employees and potential clients will be drawn to your products and services.

Being honest and built on integrity may mean making tough and uncertain decisions. However, that vulnerability will lead to important and necessary growth.

Connectivity And The Las Vegas Effect

Rule 3: Give The People What They Want

When tourists visit Las Vegas, they aren't looking for a casino that has limited operating hours. They want the full experience, and Las Vegas has given them just that with 24/7 access to everything. Las Vegas gave the consumer what it wanted, a constant nightlife that never closes or goes on vacation.

Your firm need not be open 24/7 but it needs to give the modern consumer what it wants, and that is constant

contact. A website and an email aren't enough anymore. With the advent of socially connected applications and

mobile messaging services, consumers want to connect with their brands and services after hours. The 9 – 5

availability is dead.

Twitter is 24/7. Instagram is 24/7. Facebook is 24/7. Your customers want to be able to message, schedule, and communicate with your firm when it is convenient for them, not just for you. It is significant to understand that the availability of a firm directly affects how much trust and brand loyalty consumers hold for it. If a firm makes it difficult for consumers to reach out, then they won't ever reach out.

However, if a firm makes it easy to communicate comments, questions, or concerns, the consumer will be preferentially drawn to that accessibility. So, instead of wasting after hours support, you will be converting new clients and customers.

Chapter 16: Gen Z In The Workplace

This Isn't Your Parent's Workforce

By the end of 2020, Gen Z is predicted to make up almost a quarter of the workforce. This means that as your company hires each new position, twenty-five percent of those positions will be held by an individual in their young twenties. This is a significant deal considering the corporate expectations of the Gen Z employee are different than that of the older generations like the Baby Boomers and Gen X.

Gen Z grew up watching their parents commit to a company job. It wasn't about self-growth or self-worth but hard work and trust that in time everything would work out. They watched their parents and grandparents accept that work wasn't about fulfillment or happiness but committing to a brand, a corporate entity, hoping those managers would take care of them. Gen Z watched as their parents stayed low on the totem pole, never advanced, and generally stayed a cog in a never-ending grinding clock.

Gen Z learned from this that with one life to live, they won't give that life to the company. They will keep it for themselves and their family. So, instead of companies

having the expectation that people will always want to work for them. They need to understand there are plenty of corporate positions out there. So, then tell Gen Z why yours is the best and why yours is the only choice for their

personal growth and fulfillment.

Be A Tech Forward Company

The Bay Area in California isn't just popular because of the climate and great food. The start-up culture is redefining the integration of technology and the workplace. They are breaking the mold by assuming that anything can be improved with the latest technology and seek that advancement as the key to corporate growth.

Granted, not all companies are multi-million dollar start-ups. But, honestly, if you are going to be seen as an innovative firm leaning into the future not catching up, you must pursue the adoption of tech-driven work aids. This means technology that aids the employee in doing their jobs. Whether it is an App or mobile browser application or even remote desktop technology, tech is the future and Gen Z knows no other life without it.

Critic, Review, and Support Continued Learning Constantly

Because technology evolves, grows, and changes at hyper-speeds Gen Z has made it a personal trait to learn on the fly as new experiences and technologies emerge. If they aren't doing something right, then they can't advance or grow. If they aren't advancing and growing, then they feel they will be left behind. If you are going to keep a strong Gen Z workforce active and alter you can no longer rely on just throwing them into the deep end and coming back at their quarterly review.

They will help grow a firm only if they are mentored, critiqued, reviewed, and supported along the way. Give them ample opportunity to take classes, grow professionally, and attend conferences. Innovation breeds expertise and creativity. All good things for a company's bottom line.

Develop the Experience of Being Hired

But what about the problem of getting them through the door, to begin with? How do you even attract the Gen Z workforce to your firm for even the possibility of an application? Don't rely on name recognition to make it happen. Don't expect eight sentence job descriptions and underdeveloped employment pages.

Gen Z wants the Apple, Amazon, or Google experience, not because they think that they deserve it. They don't believe that every company should roll out the red carpet as if they were the star of a movie attending the premiere in Hollywood. Gen Z is attracted to digital content that works. Apple, Amazon, and Google are all tech companies that make digital products that work. Their websites aren't just pathetic listings of aged jobs without a sense of culture. Corporate websites that don't offer the career experience but rather simple and confusing listings are more akin to ordering food from a menu that only has pictures.

Who knows if it's real or not or even what it is? Make your HR website shine. Develop a digital experience that truly and honestly describes not only the job but the company. Though, you can't use fluff words. Instead, share videos of colleagues, do onsite tours, and job fairs at your location. Allow Gen Z applicants to explore the different career paths for themselves. This gives them a sense of control and choice instead of pigeonholing.

Employ Creative Workforce Benefits

A simple 401K is not going to attract a Gen Z workforce or keep one. Gen Z doesn't want to wait until retirement to enjoy their lives. Remember they are not giving the company their life. They are giving themselves their lives. So, be the firm that supports this work-life balance. Be the firm that develops alternative benefits that support travel, home services, mental health care, and alternative health practices.

Ever think about giving your employees unlimited vacation days? Many Bay Area companies have employed this as a benefit. If you treat your employees like individuals, then they will treat your firm as if they owned a part of its success. They will take responsibility for their efforts. You don't have to treat them like family. Gen Z wants to be recognized as an individual, a person with independent thoughts, feelings, and desires, not as a cog or just a worker.

Listen and Accept That Change Is Inevitable

The most critical point about having a Gen Z workforce is to focus on their input. Gen Z will learn and grow if allowed, but they will learn and grow to benefit everyone around them. This includes your firm. They don't just want to be smarter they want to work more effectively and

efficiently. They want to develop new techniques and use creativity to solve impossible problems. Listen and support these ideas. Your firm will benefit from their exploration because they understand where the world is going. So, the final question then is: are you going with them?

Chapter 17: Millennials in the Workforce: How to Attract Them, How to Keep Them Happy

We hear entirely too much about the negative aspects of Millennials. However, they now make up the largest

segment of the workforce. We would do well to remember that every generation has been criticized by previous

generations, only to make their own unique mark on the economy. Financial advisor Dave Ramsey has said that Millennials are great but fall into two categories: they are either participation trophy-winning brats living in their

parents' basements or they are one of the most creative and driven generations ever (paraphrased).

Data seem to agree. Employers would do well to tap into this labor rich resource. While many of the negative characteristics people often complain about may prove an irritant to others, these traits are tied to their strengths. It is much wiser to see what is important to them and nurture these values to gain the mutual benefits.

Give them a reason to be loyal.

Loyalty is a virtue and has, in times past, been considered something automatically due an employer simply for the privilege of being employed by them. Older generations may even be taken aback at the suggestion that loyalty must be earned. Millennials don't necessarily think loyalty is invaluable. They simply think it can be misplaced. They grew up in a time of instability and need more assurance.

They also see employment as a relationship where both the company and the employee are benefitting. Because of this, they see no reason to stay with one company long term.

Most don't even plan on staying for more than five years at one company. They aren't really looking for special treatment, however. They just want to know that they have the benefits they value and are valued themselves. And they want to know they are doing something important.

Let them in on the vision.

The reason behind what they do is very important. Not only does knowing why things are done a certain way give them a sense of purpose, a motivator in itself, but it also empowers them to make better real-time decisions. A company may have protocols in place to address every conceivable situation, but life doesn't fit in a box and letting them in on the whys of what they do empowers them to be more proactive. It also allows them to think creatively. This may be scary for managers but taking the reins off addresses another important factor for this generation.

Give them flexibility.

And be flexible with the term flexible. They want flexibility in many ways. After all, they grew up in an educational environment that valued developing their own ideas and seeking their own directions. Autonomy has been fostered and they like it. This is a good thing. They also tend to be hands-on learners so they want the freedom to make

decisions and also the freedom to try new things and learn from their mistakes. Micromanagers are pariahs to every generation and a death knell to businesses, anyway.

Give them choices.

The flexibility they desire flows over into other areas as well. They want to be in control of their life choices, which means control over their work choices. They value experiences over possessions and they want the freedom to pursue these experiences. They want an optimal work-life balance and they have some things going for them that previous generations didn't. We all now have much more sophisticated technology that has enabled the greatest number of people to work remotely.

Sitting behind a desk for 8 hours a day, 5 days a week seems unnecessary to many Millennials, and many have good reason to ask for flexibility in this. Since they are already more autonomous and like being trusted to do their jobs, it makes sense to let them work where they want to if their job responsibilities allow for it. Besides, it would ultimately reduce the company's electric bill to let them use their own outlets to power their computers. This also allows for other areas of flexibility.

Who wouldn't want to work in their shorts or yoga pants? While this has traditionally been more the vision for many a writer, it is not so lofty a goal for others now that tele-commuting has become more prevalent. However, even those without the freedom to work from anywhere, they still value a comfortable work environment.

Office culture has been changing over the years as the in-coming workforce has gravitated towards being more re-laxed and even fun. Young people see photos of offices with bean bag chairs, game consoles in the break rooms, and even slides to get to lower floors. The environment just feels relaxed. This is due to one stark contrast of millenni-als with previous generations.

They are results-oriented.

All of the things mentioned before were foreshadowing this point. They don't care how something gets done as long as it gets done and gets done well. They want to know that they are doing a good job and that it matters. Because of this, they want to be acknowledged for the work they do. It is a mental checkmark to know that they are on track, which is where they find fulfillment. One thing employers would do well to consider is creating new titles for stages between promotions. These will give them a sense of

accomplishment and progress. It also feeds their desire for responsibility.

Adopt a culture of giving back. This sense of responsibility extends into the community. Just as they want to know that their contributions matter to their careers, they want what they do to matter to society as well. This means they want their careers to benefit society and they want the companies they work for to directly affect society.

In short, Millennials want connectedness. They want to be connected to their companies, to their colleagues, and to their communities. They want to work together for every-one's benefit and the benefits are mutual for all involved.

Chapter 18:

The Future of Marketing

The mass adoption of the internet into everyday life is the biggest event that has affected marketing over the last three decades. Since then, technology has evolved at speeds that were unimaginable 30 years ago.

With the growth of technology, the world of marketing has had to grow and adapt at a similar breakneck speed.

Marketers often feel like they're scrambling to keep up with changing algorithms and evolving technologies.

And a lot of marketers are failing to keep up. Instead of implementing changes and testing, they find one thing that works and keep repeating it. Unfortunately, the world of marketing is constantly changing, so the same old strategies won't work forever. Marketers must adapt.

Staying ahead of trends becomes extremely important in an environment like this. So, now, we will discuss some of the emerging trends in marketing so you can plan them into your campaigns ASAP.

I will mention about 7 marketing trends that can help you build powerful marketing campaigns that actually convert in 2020.

Marketing Trends to Watch

Experiences

Experiential marketing has been having its moment for a few years now with no signs of stopping any time soon. More brands are hiring marketers who know how to create experiences for their customers. Why? Because people love an Instagrammable event!

If marketers create a reason for people to show up, interact with the brand, and create content to share on social media it's a win for the brand a win for the customer. These types of marketing events also help to create good feelings between the brand and the customer, which can lead to better customer retention in the long run.

That's why "31% of marketers believe live events are the most effective marketing strategy over email marketing, content marketing, and digital advertising" and "77% of marketers use experiential marketing as a core part of their advertising strategy". Because it works!

Living in the age of Instagram, nothing is more valuable for a brand's marketing than likes, tags, and shares. By creating beautiful, Instagrammable, and branded spaces that customers can experience, you create a lasting memory for the customer and generate buzz around your brand. If experiential marketing isn't on your list for 2020, I highly recommend that changes.

Now let's talk about the next trend...

Community

Nothing speaks to the power of community to influence purchase decisions like social media. An ODM Group study found that 74% of consumers rely on social networks to help with their purchasing decisions. Another study found that 71% of people are more likely to make purchases based on social media referrals.

Communities are powerful, people! If you are not leveraging your community, think of the best way to create one now.

Facebook groups, forums, and message boards are where like-minded people can connect, discover new products to fuel their passions, and problem-solve together.

As the popularity of pay-to-participate Facebook groups increase, you'll start to see this trend amplify. Membership only sites are marketing their community aspect as a selling point: with this membership, you'll join hundreds of other people just like Y O U. It's a powerful sales tool and it's converting people into customers.

By creating a community around your brand, you're creating greater value for the customer. Now they have somewhere to share their passion for bike riding, running, scrapbooking, or whatever drives your customer. Think of the Nike Run Club.

For those of you unfamiliar with it, it's an app that Nike puts out that provides audio-guided runs and a community of runners you can "run" with and share your progress with. It's great...for Nike. Because every time there's a new audio-guided run, the Nike logo shows up on my watch. Pretty genius, huh?

Nike is leveraging this very helpful content for their fans and delivering it directly to them. It's not relying on me to find it on Facebook or to open an email. Nike can now push through the noise and come directly as a notification because of the community it created.

By creating a community for your fans to connect, you're creating a group of highly marketing qualified leads. These people are your super fans. Doesn't it makes sense to create a place where you can talk to them directly?

Inclusion

Community is part of a very important marketing strategy that you've been seeing everywhere without really realizing it: Inclusion. This is a trend that came out of the social con-sciousness of our times.

Most memorably, I think of this through a Dove campaign from a few years ago that showed a woman removing her

t-shirt to become a woman of another color. Although the order in which the women were presented caused some controversy for Dove, the message was meant to be

inclusion.

Inclusion means adding in people not typically represented in marketing. This means people of color, women of color, and the differently abled. These are all groups of people who feel marginalized and under-represented. By now

including representations of them in marketing, these

campaigns are making them feel included — and by

extension, opening up new or untapped markets.

Digital

We all know that digital marketing is here to stay,

especially as we become more and more reliant on our

screens. As technology develops to keep us ever-connected,

the digital marketing space will have to continue to evolve

and meet people where they are on their purchase journey.

Does this mean that traditional marketing is dead?

No. Traditonal marketing still has its place. With digital

marketing tools like MailChimp offering physical mail

options, we can see marketers thinking outside of the

screen. By connecting with fans in unexpected places, like

their mailbox, it can help your brand stand out from the

crowd.

Like we saw with experiential marketing, brands are trying

harder than ever to stand out and create memorable mo-

ments for their fans. Sending a piece of mail or buying ad

space at the local grocery stores are marketing methods that have been forgotten, creating a space for marketers to cheaply reach their target audiences.

Audio

The number one biggest trend in the marketing industry is voice search. With the popularity of audio assistants like the Echo, the brands optimizing for voice search are going to be the ones with a leg up next year.

And this trend isn't just important for retailers; if you're a content producer or a publisher, this trend can have a huge impact on your search results and ultimately your traffic.

If you haven't already started thinking about how to

optimize your brand for voice search, you're falling behind. Prioritize this for next year.

But I can't wrap up talking about audio without mentioning podcasts and the podcast revolution. If you think radio died, then podcasts are what rose from the ashes. A statistic from 2018 claims that "76.8% of people listen to podcasts for more than 7 hours each week."

If you're not advertising on or creating your own podcasts, this is a great opportunity for next year.

Bite-sized Content

If you're a marketer, then you know that you have about 3 seconds to grab someone's attention. If you don't grab them in that time, they're already off to the next thing.

With the constant stream of new content to consume, it's becoming harder and harder to keep people's attention, so keeping content short and to the point can be the difference between a sale and losing their interest.

While long-form content is still important, it's more important to extend the life of each piece of content by breaking them down into bite-sized and easy to digest chunks.

That's exactly why you see so many sped up videos for how-to content. These shorter pieces make it more likely that the consumer will commit to the content.

Think about it. Instagram gives you only 60 seconds for video clips (unless it's IGTV) and 15 seconds for stories. For people growing up in an Instagram era, they're used to and most comfortable with short and sweet.

Of course, there are always exceptions to the rule.

Live Video

It's no secret that video has quickly become the king of content online. It's hard to open any app or website without engaging with some kind of video content. Our Facebook and Instagram feeds are constant streams of video, not to mention the new TV shows and movies that have turned both social media platforms into networks in their own right.

So creating bite-sized video content is a given, but what about live video?

Live video is definitely having its moment right now, as you can see by the constant push from practically every social media channel to go live now. Like it's not creepy enough that they're listening to us all the time, now they want us to turn on the cameras for them too? Sheesh!

All joking aside, live video will still be a large part of the marketing strategy in the future, especially since it ties together a lot of the trends we talked about already. With live video, it's easy to create a sense of community because everyone is watching and interacting in real-time. It's also easy to create an experience for your customers they won't easily forget. You can also help make people feel included by calling out their names or including a Q&A feature.

Live video is the fastest and easiest way for a brand to connect with their audience directly from anywhere in the world. This makes it a very powerful marketing tool since marketing is all about creating connections between brands and customers.

Conclusion

So, what have we learned about the future of marketing? Yes, it's an ever-evolving industry so staying on top of emerging trends will always be a challenge. However, when you break down marketing to its core, you can see that in the end marketing is about connecting with people.

Why is experiential marketing a successful marketing strategy? Because it's an opportunity to connect with people face to face. It's an opportunity to see real faces behind a brand, not just logos. It's an opportunity to connect.

Why does live video work so well at converting sales?

Because people love having the opportunity to ask

questions live and directly interact with a brand. This helps

to build trust between the brand and customer who then

becomes a repeat customer.

You see? The end goal of marketing is simple, it's to

connect to people in a real way. If your marketing strategy

plans to connect with people, then your marketing team is

looking to the future of marketing and you'll always be

ahead of the curve.

Chapter 19: Five Next Level Marketing Strategies

As a business owner, you are always looking for ways to grow your business, reach more people, and make more money. The best way to do this is, of course, through marketing.

Marketing is absolutely vital to any successful business. It helps you reach more people who could benefit from your products and/or services. It allows you to inform them about you and what you do. It can even open up conversations between you and your prospective clients.

All of this helps to get you more clients. Those clients then spread the word about you and reach more clients, and so on. So marketing is very helpful for growing your profit.

There are a lot of great marketing strategies out there.

Email marketing is one of the most popular and successful.

You can partner with other businesses or even collaborate

with influencers. And these will help to grow your

business, but only to a certain extent.

Some marketing strategies are more advanced and build on

top of strategies you already have in place. They can help

to grow your business when other strategies seem to have

capped out. These are some of those strategies.

1. VIP Experiences

Many companies and brands host live events where they in-

vite consumers, shareholders, prospects, and others in-

volved in the company to come have a fun night together.

This is part of experiential marketing, meaning that the

people involved get to actually experience and interact with

the brand in person.

A VIP experience could be a part of one of these events that is just for VIPs, or it could be its own event entirely. Either way, having a VIP experience is a great way to get the right people involved in your company or brand.

Most VIP experiences are invite-only or require approval from the host. This is to ensure that the right people are getting the experience; the people who are or could be the most important to your brand. However, you could also open up a VIP experience to anyone, and have it cost more than the regular experience. Both will get you what you want: people who are involved in or want to be involved in your brand.

Whether you have a VIP experience has its own event or part of an existing one, there are a few things you can do to ensure that it is a success.

Online Engagement

Almost everyone is online these days. The internet is one of the largest ways for brands to interact with consumers. So it makes sense that online is also a great place to boost your event's attendance and success.

First comes the buildup. This is the stage before the actual event when you get people interested and excited to come. If you are having open ticket sales, this is the time to try and boost them. You can send evites, tease special guests or speaker lineups, and create regular posts about important dates or deadlines. This will help to get more people interested and boost your ticket sales.

There are other things you can do online as well. You can offer sneak peeks backstage on platforms like Snapchat, Instagram, and Facebook. This will give attendees a feeling of greater inclusion in the event.

You can also interact with the audience before and during the event. You can create live polls or ask questions, so consumers can give their feedback and opinions.

Communication

Communication between your brand and your consumers is key. It will make the attendees feel heard and help you communicate what your brand is all about and what you would like from your consumers.

A spokesperson is a great way of advertising your brand, both online and in person. This can be a person professionally trained in your company, or it can be a celebrity.

Brand ambassadors are another great and vital option. They will be touched on later in this article.

A good emcee is also very important. This person will do most of the talking to the crowd. They can read the crowd's mood and energy levels and help to build on that and give attendees a great and memorable experience. They can work to deliver your brand's message and keep audience members engaged.

VIP experiences are a great way to grow interest in your brand from the right people. These are the people who will provide you with the most support, and hopefully, profit. Adding a VIP section to your event or hosting a separate VIP event is a tried and true marketing strategy for your business.

2. Memberships

Almost everybody is a member of something. Sam's Club, the library, a magazine, a gym, etc. People love feeling like they are a part of something, which is why memberships are so popular. This is what makes memberships a fantastic marketing tool to increase the involvement of your business and your profit.

Virtually any business can benefit from some form of membership program. There are a lot of benefits of marketing programs for business, including:

- **An increase in customer loyalty**: if customers feel like they belong to your brand, they will feel loyal to you

- **Provides a steady stream of revenue**: rather than selling goods or services occasionally, a membership program provides you with a constant and reliable source of revenue

- **Brings more revenue from existing customers**: people who are satisfied will want to move up to higher levels, bringing more money

- **Improves referrals:** customers who enjoy being a member are more likely to encourage other people to join as well

- **Sells more stuff easier:** Products and services can be included in membership benefits, so you sell easier. And customers will be more likely to purchase more of your products or services

The benefits of a membership program are tremendous. Here are a few things to remember if you want to have a membership program for your business.

Levels of memberships

Many membership programs, especially for large brands and companies, have multiple levels to them. The different levels available depend on the type of business and their preferences, but they all have a few things in common.

First, rewards get greater as membership levels get higher. This is just common sense. The more someone pays to be a member, the more they want to get out of it. This can also give them a greater sense of loyalty because they feel like they are more valued.

Additionally, the benefits can't be things available to

normal customers. If so, no one will want to pay to be a

member.

If you have a smaller business, you may only want to

provide one level of membership. That is perfectly fine.

What's important is that the customer feels like they are

gaining perks, growing their sense of loyalty to your

business.

Pricing

Again, this one is mostly up to your preferences. Higher

membership levels will cost more money. You can price

your membership however you want. Just make sure that

the customer feels they are getting their money's worth.

A smart idea is to make the lowest tier of membership very

affordable. This way a lot of people will want to join, and

eventually want to move to a higher membership. It is a

way to easily get people involved while still providing you

with profit. And even if the price is low, as long as it isn't free members will feel like they made an important commitment.

Keeping members

Renewal is one of the greatest challenges of memberships. It's hard to keep people interested long enough they want to keep paying. But there are two great ways to do this: offer incentives; and go above your promises.

Incentives like discounts on renewal will make customers want to renew more because they will feel like they're getting more out of it.

Going above and beyond what you promise will certainly keep customers coming back for more. They will get what they're paying for, and then some, so they will feel like there is a strong benefit to renewing.

A membership program is a great way to build customer loyalty and provide a steady stream of profit. It is one of the best marketing tools for your business if you already have a decent customer base.

3. Brand Ambassadors

Brand ambassadors are, as the name suggests, people who advertise and talk about your brand. We see this often with celebrities or influencers who are paid to advertise a brand. This works great because these ambassadors have large followings, so they are more likely to convert people.

However, while this is helpful, you don't have to pay for ambassadors like this to be successful.

The best ambassadors are your employees and your

customers. Customers, though, often act as ambassadors on their own, even without thinking about it. These are called "organic" ambassadors. If people like your business, products, and/or services, then they are likely to talk about them.

These organic ambassadors are sharing real feelings and opinions, so they often convert at least a few people. And all you have to do is make them like your brand.

So the ambassadors you should be focusing on are your employees. Here's why.

Availability

You probably already have employees. This means you don't have to hire more just to be ambassadors. No interviews, no resumes, no long and tiring processes. You have everyone you need right in front of you.

This is why employees make great choices for ambassadors. It is easy for you to have them fill the role without extra time. It also saves on expenses, because you don't have to hire a new person or new people to do a job that your current employees can do.

Outreach

Being a brand ambassador does not require hours of commitment, planning, and work. All it takes is for you to share something about your brand to gain more customers— on social media, in person, or through other means.

This means that each and every one of your employees could be an ambassador. All they have to do is make a post on their social media advertising services, products, features, job openings, etc.

The more employees you have, the more successful this will be. Let's pretend that each employee who acts as an ambassador converts five new customers, even though this number can be much higher. That means for 100 employees, there are 500 new customers.

Having your employees act as ambassadors can be

incredibly successful in converting new customers and

reaching more people.

Cost efficiency

Targeted, pay-per-click ads are used often. They can do a

great job of converting more customers. But ambassadors

are often more successful and cost much less.

People are more likely to be interested in a brand or busi-

ness if it is being talked about by someone they know. This

is why brand ambassadors are often more successful than

ads because of the personal connection.

And, ambassadors cost a lot less. Your employees could all

act as ambassadors without having to pay any extra fees or

costs.

You may have to pay for some sort of platform to organize and boost your ambassadors' efforts. Even so, this will be much cheaper and more efficient than paying for ad space.

Brand ambassadors are a simple and cost-efficient way to grow your business and reach more customers. They can have incredible outreach at a very low cost, which is what makes having brand ambassadors such a great marketing strategy.

4. Personalized Interactions

As the marketing world changes, customers change as well. Customers no longer want to be seen as a point of data, but as a real person. It has been shown that customers who feel like a company knows them are far more likely to purchase from that company.

This is what makes personalized interactions such a great marketing strategy. Personalized marketing is taking data from customers and using it to have conversations, send leads, and offer bonuses tailored specifically to that client.

Personalized marketing has many benefits, including:

2. **Better customer experiences**: if customers feel that their experience is personalized to them, they will enjoy it more. This also means they are more likely to purchase because they are happier with their experience.

3. **Better understanding of visitors**: the more data you collect, the more you will understand what your customers are like. This allows you to tailor your goods and services to fit the demand.

4. **Increased brand loyalty:** as with memberships, personalized marketing makes customers feel like they are a part of something. This will make them more loyal to your brand.

5. **Increased revenue:** *happier customers* means more purchases. So personalized marketing will help to drive up your revenue.

Personalized marketing has a lot of benefits. But how exactly does it work?

It starts with data collection. There are many ways you can do this. You can track purchase history for each of your customers. You can also use browser history, email submissions, SMS information, and more to gather personalized information for each of your clients.

Be careful when doing this, though. It is always best to ask a customer's permission before collecting their data. This is why so many websites notify you they use cookies and that by entering their site, you are permitting them to do this. You can also use different types of opt-ins to get the permission of your customers.

Once you have customer data, the next step is creating personalized interactions. This can be done through a variety of ways. You can make sure that conversations with them are tailored to their needs and wants. You can offer them products you think they will like, deals on those products, and even send emails about abandoned carts.

Doing all of this manually is nearly impossible. It's simply too much for one person, or even a team of people, to handle. That's why automated services are great for personalized marketing.

There are many automated and AI services out there to help you with personalized marketing. Not every one will work for you, though, so find one that can do what you want.

Personalized marketing helps customers feel seen by a company and increases their brand loyalty. It helps to drive up your revenue and even improves customer retention. So, this is a great marketing strategy that will surely help you grow your business.

5. Gated Offers

Gated offers are similar to personalized interactions because they are formulated so it attempts to make a customer feel seen as an individual. Gated offers can take two forms, either as content or offers and promotions. Let's look at each.

Gated content is content that a customer must do something to obtain. This does not mean the customer is buying the content. Gated offers do not require money.

A popular form of gated content is eBooks or whitepapers that are available if you give the distributor some contact information. This can be as simple as filling out a form with your email and name and receiving a free eBook. But as a business, you can ask for more information from your customers. This can include addresses, phone numbers, age, sex, and virtually any other information.

Gated offers work similarly. The customer inputs the desired information, and they are given a coupon or a special offer.

Some gated offers require eligibility. For example, you could offer discounts to teachers, veterans, or college students. Customers could put in information that verifies they fit into that category, and then they are given the offer.

Having gated content and offers has a lot of benefits for your business. Let's go over some of them.

More personalized information

When you get this kind of information from your customers, you learn more about them. This helps you to create personalized content, like what was discussed with personalized marketing. It also helps you to know who your customers are, so you can change your practices to fit their wants better.

Greater customer retention

Customers who receive these kinds of offers feel like they have made some sort of agreement with your brand. This increases their loyalty and the chance they will keep coming to you. Again, if they feel like they belong, then they will keep coming back.

Gated offers and content are not always the best option for you. They can boost customer loyalty and retention, yes. But if every piece of content you have is gated, customers are less likely to want it.

Find a balance of gated and non-gated content. Provide your customers with some content, or even offers they can access with no commitment from them. This can be a blog, case studies, infographics, and more.

Once a customer has seen some ungated content, then they are more likely to want more from your business. This is when gated content and offers are useful: it offers them more of what they like at a small cost from them.

Gated offers have their benefits and downsides. However, if used right, they can be a great way to boost your customer loyalty and revenue. This is why gated offers are one of the best marketing strategies out there when used carefully.

Wrapping Up

Marketing your business can be difficult and tiresome. You want, even need, to grow your customer base and your profits. But some of the basic strategies have stopped bringing you more success.

This is when next-level marketing strategies like the ones here are helpful. They will build on your client base and help you to drive up your revenue and improve client interactions. Trying these five marketing strategies will surely bring good results for your business.

www.ingramcontent.com/pod-product-compliance
Lightning Source LLC
Chambersburg PA
CBHW021800190326
41518CB00007B/383